The Essence oɪ ᴋᴇɪᴋɪ
A Complete Guide To 1st & 2nd Degree

Garry & Adele Malone

Dedicated
to
Kim Buckley

The Essence of Reiki
A Complete Guide To 1st & 2nd Degree

REIKI
The Usui Method of Natural Healing

Garry & Adele Malone

Tranceformational Seminars & Publications
Tel/Fax: 01923 245181 e:mail garry.malone@virgin.net

Tranceformational Seminars & Publications
2 Talbot Avenue Watford Herts WD1 4AX
Tel\Fax : 01923 245181
e-mail : garry.malone@virgin.net

First Published in the UK
by Tranceformational Seminars & Publications in April 1998

Second Printing in July 1998
Third Printing in September 1998

We have made every effort to acknowledge all the source material and to secure permission
from copyright holders when required. In the event of any question arising as to the source of
any material we will be pleased to make the necessary acknowledgement in future printing.

A Catalogue record for this book
is available from the British Library

ISBN 0 9532620 0 6

Printed and bound in Great Britain by
Antony Rowe Ltd, Chippenham, Wiltshire

" Man extols God as omnipresent, omniscient and omnipotent, yet he ignores His presence in himself!
God is in the heart of every human being...
All men are cells in the divine organism."

Sri Sathya Sai Baba

Authors & Publishers Disclaimer

Reiki is a form of healing that has been used by the authors and countless other practitioners. The information and techniques in this book do not constitute medical advice. Healing and medicine are two very different disciplines. You should always remember to seek medical advice from a qualified doctor or practitioner in the case of serious illness.

Acknowledgements

Garry Malone would like to thank

Tricia Courtney-Dickens my Reiki Master/Teacher, for her wonderful ability to teach with such clarity and for passing on this gift of healing.

Kim Buckley my beautiful and inspirational sister who died of Cancer at the age of 33. Her love of life and positive attitude continues to inspires me and my family. The tragedy of her death made me realise how precious life is, and I have dedicated my life to healing and teaching.

Garry & Adele Malone would like to thank

Our four children Molly, Harriette-Rose, Charlotte and Garry, your love, help, enthusiasm and support are a constant inspiration. Finally special thanks to Kim Scudder for her wonderful drawings and illustrations.

CONTENTS

THE FIRST DEGREE

THE SECOND DEGREE

IMPORTANT NOTE TO
THE READER / STUDENT

The purpose of this book is to give the reader a comprehensive guide to the teachings and disciplines associated with first and second degree Reiki. We have purposely kept the information concise so the reader can quickly and easily understand and apply Reiki. Wherever possible we have avoided adding personal beliefs that may differ from the traditional teachings of Dr Mikao Usui. The knowledge and information contained in this book is based on the original Shiki Rhoyo Method of Healing developed by Dr Usui almost two hundred years ago.

If you desire to use these teachings to heal yourself and others you must first receive the necessary attunements in person from a Reiki Master. This book should be kept with you as a constant reference guide. The *Free CD* - Heartbeat has been specially composed to be used for meditation and healing. Reiki Masters can purchase copies of this book, including *Free CD* at special rates if they wish to use and distribute it in their own workshops by contacting Garry Malone on 01923 245181 0r e-mail garry.malone@virgin.net

SPECIAL ACKNOWLEDGEMENT
AND RESPECT TO OUR REIKI LINEAGE

Our Reiki Family Tree

Doctor Mikao Usui

Doctor Chujiro Hayashi

Hawayo Takata

Iris Ishikuro

Arthur Robertson

Rick & Emma Ferguson

Margarette L. Shelton

Kathleen Ann Milner

Robert N. Wachsberger

Tricia Courtney Dickens

Garry Malone

Adele Malone

INTRODUCTION
by
Garry Malone

Reiki is the gift of vitally and self preservation encoded into the genetic makeup of all God's creatures. It is the higher self's connection to the universal energy that breathes life into all living things. We are all born with the omniscient wisdom to heal and preserve life. All living things are connected. Our ancestors used and relied on their own abilities and instincts. Unfortunately, these basic skills have been forgotten and are rarely used today. Humanity in its relentless ambition for progress has given up its most precious and natural gift.

Through the media and clever advertising campaigns the majority of the world's population have been conditioned to rely heavily on modern technology at the expense of their own birthright. There is a need for humanity to become re-balanced. Instead of giving up responsibility for one's life and health, it is vitally important to regain an equilibrium between ancient and modern technology. Reiki is the catalyst.

Many people believe when you are ready to embrace the principles of Reiki you will be guided to a teacher. I personally believe that Reiki with its infinite wisdom and unconditional love seeks out the person when they need it most. This is true of my own experience and introduction to Reiki.

Like many people in the healing profession I was inspired to help others through personal tragedy. My sister Kim Buckley died of Cancer at the young age of thirty-three, leaving behind a devastated husband, four young children and a large family. During her brief attempt to beat cancer she asked me to help her fight against this horrible disease. With no real knowledge of medicine or complementary therapies I searched for hope. Doctors and nurses were unable and unwilling to offer any encouragement, refusing to step outside the realms of modern medicine. We were told to just accept that she was going to die. Modern medicine gave up exposing its limitations.

Angry and frustrated at the hospitals cold, blunt diagnosis I began to search bookshops for inspiration. Love, Medicine and Miracles a wonderful book by Dr Bernie Siegel jumped out at me. It told of a more compassionate and holistic approach to diseases such as cancer and aids. There were stories of people who survived even after being told there was no hope. It explained how by taking responsibility for your own health and future you could fight back if you wished. Even in death you could have control and dignity.

Dr Siegel, an oncologist had become disillusioned with the way he had been taught to treat his patients. After attending a seminar on guided imagery he decided to developed and pioneer an alternative approach. In 1978, Dr Siegel set-up a therapy programme called ECAP (Exceptional Cancer and Aids Patients). Since then he has established centres throughout the USA. This book and Dr Siegel's work inspired me to change my life. My new path began with the study of the mind through Hypnosis and NLP (Neuro Linguistic Programming).

Fortunately for me, while I was training in Hypnotherapy and NLP I met a lady called Tricia Courtney-Dickens who introduced me to Reiki. Her enthusiasm for this ancient art of healing was infectious. I decided to enrol in her next Reiki course to study the first degree. That weekend workshop changed my perceptions of holistic healing. Reiki put me in touch with my natural abilities to heal myself and others, I was amazed by Reiki's subtle yet profound power.

Let's Share Our Love & Make A More Beautiful World

Let's take every opportunity to share our LOVE by being kind, friendly, considerate, patient, understanding, thoughtful, respectful & helpful with each other.

Let's accept each other just as we are.

Let's promote harmony & goodwill
by refusing to criticise or gossip.

Let's be first to let go of hurt feelings &
hold forgiveness in our hearts.

Let's agree to disagree in agreeable ways &
make our differences OK. with each other.

Let's comunicate our misunderstandings &
be above holding grudges.

Let's be tolerant of each others faults & look
to find only the good in each other.

Let's look for what we can appreciate about each
other & let's lift each other by sharing what
we appreciate about each other.

Let's smile at each other, & be good listeners.

LOVE is the answer. Let's share our LOVE today !

Author Unknown

❖ 6 ❖

REIKI

THE FIRST DEGREE

Whatever you can do,
or dream you can,
begin it.
Boldness has genius,
power and magic in it,
Begin it now.

- Goethe

CHAPTER 1

UNIVERSAL LIFE FORCE

In The Beginning

There is a non physical ubiquitous energy that gives life to every living organism. For many thousands of years we have known of this energy and have sought to develop ways to harness its power to heal and influence our lives. The Japanese call this energy Ki. It is also known as Chi by the Chinese, Prana by some Asian cultures and the Holy Spirit or Holy Ghost by most of the western world.

We carry this energy in and around our bodies from the moment we are conceived. Science has established its existence, and with the aid of Kirlian photography we are able to see this energy that encompasses all living things. Ancient Eastern cultures have been applying this energy for healing since before the birth of Jesus Christ. Many successful disciplines such as Reiki, Tai Chi, Feng Shui, Meditation, Yoga and Acupuncture have been developed to control and greatly enhance the flow of this energy in and around the body. The energy itself is pure and has omniscient wisdom. When it is allowed to flow unencumbered it fills the body with a profound sense of well-being, healing, repairing and rejuvenating as it goes.

Unfortunately, this gift from God has been abused and wasted by so many people for so long. We are conditioned and programmed by so many negative forces today, that we have forgotten how to use the natural abilities we all possess to make our lives fulfilling and exciting. Instead, we opt for destructive and damaging pursuits that weaken this life giving energy.

10 Things That Weaken The Life Giving Energy

- Too Much Alcohol
- A Poor Diet
- A Lack of Exercise
- Drugs
- Tobacco
- Negative Habits
- Stress
- Poor Breathing
- Lack of Sleep & Rest
- Negative Psychic Activity

Humanity has become fragmented and hollow, we are only a shadow of what we could be. We need to go back to go forward once more. By practising the discipline of Reiki you regain your natural abilities to heal yourself and others and the knowledge you require to lead a happier more fulfilling life.

Nature's life giving energy is a great and wise teacher, by pursuing its wisdom through Reiki you will grow to new heights of understanding and life will flow at a more enjoyable and exciting pace. Remember always that this life giving energy is a gift from God - your Birthright. Everyone possesses this gift and uses it daily even though they probably do not realise they are doing so.

When a child for instance falls and hurts their knee, instinctively they place their hand on the sore spot and the pain is relieved as they unconsciously work with this energy to heal themselves. Likewise, a parent will kiss their child's hurt or injured limb better and place their hand on top. Unknowingly both the parent and the child are working unconsciously with this healing energy. The parent sending and channelling the energy while the child is receiving and drawing the energy.

This wonderful energy is free. There are no patents or copyrights attached. All you need is the desire and the ***discipline*** to attune yourself to the energy and its life changing properties.

A new philosophy, a way of life,
is not given for nothing.
It has to be paid dearly for and only acquired
with much patience and great effort

Fyodor Dostoyevsky

CHAPTER 2

WHAT IS REIKI?

Reiki?

Reiki is a form of hands on healing, with it origins in India and the East dating back many thousands of years to the time before Christ and Buddha. The original name, disciplines and techniques of Reiki were lost due to the traditional method of passing knowledge from generation to generation by word of mouth. Exactly when this ancient art of healing disappeared is difficult to determine. However, we do know that it was rediscovered by a Japanese Scholar and monk name Dr Mikao Usui. It was in fact Dr Usui who fashioned the name ***REIKI.***

Reiki is a two syllable Japanese word meaning universal life force. Although the proper Japanese pronunciation is RYE-KEY, it has been westernised to RAY-KEY. Rei means universal, omnipresent — present everywhere at the same time. Esoterically Rei means spiritual consciousness, the omniscient wisdom from God or the higher self.

Ki is the non physical vitality that gives life to all living things. Many cultures understand and recognise the importance of Ki energy and how it impacts our lives and well-being. Ki energy can be activated for the purpose of healing. When you feel healthy and full of enthusiasm, the flow of Ki energy in your body is high and unencumbered. Life seems easier to deal with and you have a higher resistance to illness and disease.

However, when your KI energy is low because maybe you are under stress or feeling unhappy and tired you will be more susceptible to disease and sickness. Your attitude will be generally negative and you will find it difficult to deal with life's challenges. KI is the very essence of the soul, it leaves the body when a person dies.

Reiki is holistic, it works on the body mind and spirit by stimulating our own natural healing abilities. The blocked emotional and physical elements that lead to illness and disease are cleared. Reiki is neither positive nor negative, it is in fact the highest and most profound vibration of life. Divine in origin, it allows us all to become one with all things alive in our world. Reiki is pure unconditional love and joy bringing all who experience and embrace it principles together in harmony.

The skills and techniques associated with Reiki are simple and easy to learn. Small children and adults can equally comprehend and incorporate this ancient form of healing into their lives. Regular contact with Reiki will bring the recipients mind body and spirit into balance. It will also help prevent future creation of illness and disease.

Reiki energy will never force its way into to your mind body or spirit. It can only ever be drawn by the recipient. If you are ready to accept and embrace Reiki it will have a profound and life changing affect on you.

Reiki is free from all rules, religions and dogma, making it open to people from all walks of life. Everyone can draw on KI energy. However, it can only be accessed once a person has been attuned to it. This is only made possible through a sacred ceremony perform by a Reiki Master.

"Reiki is the greatest secret in the science of energetics"
Madam Hawayo Takata

In the deeper reality beyond space and time,
we may be all members of one body.

Sir James Jeans

CHAPTER 3

HOW REIKI WORKS

The human body is made up of over 50 trillion cells. Each cell contains omniscient wisdom and is connected to the universe and every living thing within it. A good analogy is to think of the universe as a huge ocean of water. Every living thing within that ocean is like a tiny droplet. Together these droplets make up and are part of Reiki the universal life force.

Reiki is part of our genetic structure. An in built intelligence that energises the mind body and spirit. Reiki stimulates growth, health, life and healing. When it is freely allowed to flow around the body it can keep us alive and healthy for over one hundred and twenty years.

Unfortunately, bad habits and poor choices result in the flow of Reiki being stifled. It is important to note that Reiki cannot be destroyed. Even when we die and the life force leaves our body it continues to exist as part of the universe. Through neglect and ignorance we abuse this vital component of life.

When the mind body and spirit are in harmony the biological intelligence that governs the body's resources and allows it to heal itself and function correctly are intensified. Reiki is the key that unlocks the body's optimum capabilities. There are seven main energy centres in the body that control the flow of the universal life force. They are called the Chakra's. Each chakra is responsible for supplying energy to specific parts of the body. When they are blocked or clogged the body becomes sick and the flow of energy is diluted.

A full Reiki treatment reopens the chakra's and re-balances the flow of the universal life force around the body. A person will normally need four full treatments on four consecutive days to boost the flow of Reiki energy. This will stimulate the body's immune system and natural healing abilities. Normally the body will begin by cleansing itself of toxins. As the poisons are removed, the body becomes re-balanced and the healing process can begin.

Many cultures have developed techniques and disciplines that stimulate the flow of KI energy around the body. However, Reiki is the easiest to learn and administer. The techniques are simple to master. The results are profound.

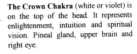

The Crown Chakra (white or violet) is on the top of the head. It represents enlightenment, intuition and spiritual vision. Pineal gland, upper brain and right eye.

The Third Eye Chakra (Indigo) is positioned in the middle of the forehead, just above the eyebrows. It represents psychic perception, telepathy and ESP. Spine, lower brain, left eye, pituitary gland, nose, ears and central nervous system.

The Throat Chakra (light blue) is positioned in the centre of the neck. It represents self expression, emotions, communication and creativity. Throat, thyroid gland, upper lungs, arms and digestive tract.

The Heart Chakra (Rose and green) is positioned in the middle of the chest. It represents emotions, love, devotion, spiritual growth and compassion. Heart, thymus gland, liver, lungs and the circulation system.

The Solar Plexus Chakra (yellow) is positioned just above the naval. It represents the centre of the body, food is assimilated, turn into energy and distributed throughout the body. Emotions, stomach, liver, digestion, gall bladder and the pancreas.

The Sacral Chakra (orange) is positioned just below the naval. It represents sexual energy, perceptions and first impressions of people. Reproductive organs, legs and the gonads.

The Root Chakra (red) is located at the genitals. It represents life, physical vitality, birth and creation. Spine, kidneys, bladder and the suprarenal glands.

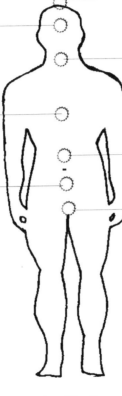

The Seven Major Chakra Points

Note: *The Chakra's are present both at the front and back of the body.*

Reiki is ever-present in our bodies. This means anyone can harness this profound inbuilt intelligent energy for healing. However, without being attuned to the universal life force you will only be using about 10-20% of its capacity for healing.

Madam Takata explained it best when she described Reiki as being similar to radio waves. We cannot see them but we know they are everywhere around us. When we turn on a radio and tune into the radio waves we can pick up a signal. That signal is turned into a radio programme. Similarly the universal life force is everywhere, although we cannot see it unless we use Kirlian photography. When we are tuned into the energy by a Reiki Master we are able to harness Reiki to heal ourselves and others. This gift of healing remains with us for the rest of our lives. We can only lose it if we use it for negative or destructive purposes. Reiki is pure and it needs to be treated as such.

Reiki is channelled through the hands. When you place your hands on your own body, or the body of another person for the purpose of healing you connect with the universal life force. The wisdom of Reiki then goes to work to bring about healing, balance and whatever is needed on a holistic level.

The best way to understand how Reiki works is to experience it.

CHAPTER 4

THE HISTORY OF REIKI

The Origins of Reiki

The Japanese like many ancient cultures used word of mouth to pass their history and practices down from generation to generation. Unfortunately this led to a great deal of knowledge and wisdom being watered down and lost. Many people involved with Reiki believe that the techniques we use today for healing were first used in India by Buddha and later by Jesus.

Others look back even further to the civilisations of Mu and Atlantis for the birth and development of Reiki. Of course without written proof we can only speculate how humanity learnt to harness and develop the universal life force. What we can be certain of and confirm is that it was rediscovered at the end of the nineteenth century by Dr Mikao Usui.

Until comparatively recently apart from the tomb of Dr Mikao Usui in Tokyo, there has been very little material evidence of his life and work. Most written accounts on the history of Reiki declare that Dr Usui was a Christian monk who lectured at Doshisha University in Kyoto. One day a student asked Dr Usui if he believed the teachings of the bible to be true. Could Jesus walk on water and heal people by touch. Audaciously he questioned if Dr Usui himself could heal the sick like Jesus.

Usui had to admit that this was beyond his capabilities. Embarrassed at being asked such questions and unable to demonstrate an answer, the story goes on to say that Doctor Usui immediately resigned his post and began a personal quest to discover how he could heal in the way that Jesus had. The legend becomes even more doubtful when it recounts how Dr Usui decided to begin his search for the secrets of healing like Jesus, in America - namely the University of Chicago.

Reiki Master William Rand has been able to disprove the legend of Dr Usui's search for enlightenment in America. Chicago University has no record of Dr Usui ever attending as a student. Further more there is no record of Dr Usui ever attending or lecturing at the Doshisha University. This work by William Rand confirms what many people believe. The history of Dr Usui's life had been changed and coloured to suit western society. Logically there are far too many holes in the legend.

The Life of Dr Mikao Usui

Mikao Usui was born into a family that had been practising Zen Buddhism for eleven generations. As a youth Usui developed a fascination for all things Western. However, he never travelled outside Japan. After leaving school he went on to study allopathic medicine with several western allopathic physicians who had graduated from Yale and Harvard University.

When a cholera epidemic spread through Tokyo, Usui was struck down with the disease. During his hospitalisation as he was close to death he had a spiritual experience. This inspired Usui to study the ancient teachings of his ancestors. He joined a Zen monastery and began reading the ancient Sanskrit and Sutras.

After many years of study Usui found references to an ancient form of healing. Further study revealed methods, formulas and symbols that detailed exactly how to practice and master this art of hands on healing. However, although he had the technical knowledge to practise healing, he lacked the wisdom to turn the teachings into reality. He needed the key to turn on and activate the power. Usui decided to seek the final piece of the jigsaw through meditation.

Taking leave from the monastery, Usui set off for the holy mountain of Kurayama. When he reached the top he picked up twenty-one pebbles and placed them in front of himself. He sat down and began his meditation. Each day he threw away one pebble. For twenty-one days he prayed, meditated, sang and read the Sutras. On the last day as he prayed he ask God to show him the light. Suddenly, a bright light appeared in the sky and came rapidly towards him, hitting him on his forehead, at the third eye chakra. Usui was knocked unconscious, and whilst in this altered state he saw a vision of the same symbols he had earlier found in the Sutras.

This vision was the confirmation Dr. Usui needed. He now knew that he had found the keys to the ancient form of healing used by Buddha and Jesus. When Usui regained full consciousness, he proceeded to return down the mountain. On his descent, he stubbed and cut his toe, he instinctively placed his hand on the toe and the bleeding and pain stopped.

On arrival at a nearby village he stopped to rest and eat.

He was able despite having fasted for 21 days, eat a healthy meal without any stomach pain. The girl who served Usui the meal was in great pain suffering from a toothache. Usui asked if he could place his hands on her swollen face, she agreed, and he was able to ease the swelling and the pain. Rested, Usui returned to the monastery. On Arrival he found his friend, the Abbot in bed suffering with severe arthritis. Once again Usui was able to alleviate the pain and suffering. Usui called this gift from God - Reiki, the Japanese word for universal life force.

These experiences became known as the four miracles. Having demonstrated his knowledge and new ability to heal the Abbott advised Usui to take this special gift into the slums of Kyoto to heal the beggars. He was reminded that it is not enough to heal the body, it is of equal importance to heal the spirit and mind also. This lesson was brought home to him very abruptly seven years later. Having spent the time giving Reiki to beggars in the slums of Kyoto to get them working, he found them returning to him with the excuse that it was easier to beg.

Usui had forgotten a basic doctrine. Mortified he re-treated to meditate once again. This time he was enlightened with the five principles of Reiki. The rest of Usui's life was spent healing, teaching and developing the Usui Shiki Rhoyo method of healing. Usui had nineteen major students who were all either western allopathic or traditional Japanese in their practice. He knew he would have to develop a method that could be understood and accepted by any religion or culture. Reiki was fashioned by Usui to have no dogma or religious beliefs attached to it. This made Reiki universal.

Tenno, the Emperor of Japan honoured Usui's work by awarding him a doctorate. By the time of his death in 1930, Dr Mikoa Usui had initiated all nineteen of his students to the level of Reiki Master/Teacher. Dr Chujiro Hayashi was chosen as the next Grand Master. It is important to note that Dr Usui taught all three degrees together. Dr Usui was cremated and his ashes placed in a Zen Monastery in Tokyo.

Dr Chujiro Hayashi

Upon the death of Dr Usui, Hayashi took over the role of Grand Master. He was responsible for training a further sixteen Reiki Masters and creating a set formula for training. Chujiro Hayashi was born into an upper class Japanese family, and was a qualified physician and retired Marine commander. He set up a clinic near the Emperors palace in Tokyo called Shina No Macha. Each day his students held healing sessions at the clinic, or visited people in their homes in they were unable to travel.

Hayashi went on to write many reports on the systems he had developed to treat various ailments. Special diets were incorporated into his treatments to assist the healing process. Probably his greatest advancement for Reiki was to discover the importance of whole body treatment and how the universal life force would go wherever it was needed to heal. Providing of course you applied the full body treatment. This was needed to remove any emotional or physical blocks.

Madam Hawayo Takata

Hawayo Kawamuru was born on the Island of Hawaii on 24th December 1900. At the age of seventeen she married Saichi Takata. They had a happy marriage with two daughters. Tragically, her husband died at the young age of thirty-two. After thirteen years of marriage Hawayo Takata was left to raise two small children on her own. The stress and pressure of the situation took toll on her health. Within five years of her husbands death she was diagnosed to be suffering from nervous exhaustion. Her health deteriorated to the point where she required surgery for a diseased gall bladder. However, she was also suffering from respiratory problems that meant the use of an anaesthetic during surgery could kill her.

This was an extremely depressing and trying time in her life. Unfortunately there was more pain and suffering to come when her sister died. As her parents had returned to live in Tokyo, it was Hawayo Takata traditional responsibility to bring the news to them in person.

After her arrival in Japan, she sought help at a hospital in Akasaka. It was discovered that she now had a tumour and appendicitis to add to her diseased gallbladder and respiratory problems. Her weight dropped dramatically and her doctor advised her to have immediate surgery.

That night as she lay in bed she heard a voice saying, "The surgery is not necessary." The next day as she was being prepared for surgery she heard the voice again saying, "The surgery was not necessary, ask, ask." Takata asked the surgeon if there was another way she could be healed and he told her of the Reiki clinic run by Dr. Hayashi. The surgeon had a sister who had been there herself and had recovered fully from an illness.

Madam Takata went to the clinic and received treatments regularly for four months and was completely healed. She decided that she also wanted to learn Reiki and set up her own practice in Hawaii. Against all tradition, she was eventually able to persuade Dr. Hayashi to allow her to work and train at the clinic for twelve months. At the end of this time it was felt that she had earned the privilege of receiving the second degree in Reiki - the practitioners level.

In the summer of 1937 Madam Takata returned to Hawaii and set up her own Reiki clinic. She spent her time healing and teaching Reiki. Dr Hayashi visited Madam Takata in February 1938 and invited her to become a Reiki Master. He said that she had gone through tests and had lived up to the Reiki Ideals and principles. She was the first woman and the first foreigner to be given this honour. Hayashi returned to Japan.

At the beginning of 1940 Japan was close to war with America. Dr Hayashi was aware he would be called up to fight. As a man of healing and peace he decided the only honourable thing to do was to precipitate his transition. He put his affairs in order. Madam Takata woke up one morning and saw a vision of

Dr Hayashi at the foot of her bed. She realised she must travel immediately to Japan. On arrival in Japan she met with Dr Hayashi and he explained his decision to leave this world. They spent many days planning the future.

When Hayashi was satisfied he had safeguarded the future of Reiki he called all his students and friends together. At this point he declared Madam Takata his successor and the third Grand Master of Reiki. Dressed in traditional Japanese attire he lay down and allowed his spirit to leave his body.Madam Takata installed as the next Grand Master returned to Hawaii to continue her teaching and healing.

This is when the history of Reiki was changed to portray Dr Mikao Usui as a Christian. Madam Takata realised that the American people and the Western world in general would hold certain bigotry towards the Japanese. So soon after the War it would be impossible to promote a method of healing with its roots firmly in Buddhism and Japan.

Madam Takata went on to train a further twenty-two Reiki Masters before her death in December 1980. There were two Grand Masters installed to continue Takata's work. Phyllis Lei Furumoto, the granddaughter of Madam Takata and Dr Bar-

bara Weber. This partnership was to run for only a year until for personal reasons they split up to continue the work separately. The Reiki Alliance was formed by Phyllis Lei Furumuto, while Dr Weber set up the A.I.R.A. (The American International Reiki Association).

Unfortunately, like many special things in this world the human ego has taken hold. There are now several different associations throughout the world all fighting amongst each other. Each claiming to have the only correct way of teaching Reiki. There is even a system of Reiki now being taught in eleven degrees. The latest rumours of an application to Copyright © Reiki seem to show how far this wonderful gift from God can be tainted.

There is only one Reiki. No-one has the right to claim it as their own, it belongs to humanity and the universe. Our only wish for the future of Reiki is that instead of fighting and bickering everyone involved with Reiki can again come together in the true spirit of healing. Let's share our experiences and skills so Reiki can be accepted universally as a natural treatment for the mind body and spirit. We need to work together to promote this cause. It is vital in our increasingly harsh and vio-

lent world that we change the whole psyche of humanity. Together we can bring this gift of healing to the world. We need
Reiki practised and used in every hospital and clinic in the
world. Let's spread the word positively. Let's make a difference.
Let's make Dr Usui, Dr Hayashi and Madam Takata Proud.
Let's honour their work and their memory. Let's live and in-
ternalise the Reiki Principles.

The Five Reiki Principles

- *Just for today I will not worry.*
- *Just for today I will not be angry.*
- *Just for today I will do my work honestly.*
- *Just for today I will give thanks for my many blessings.*
- *Just for today I will be kind to my neighbour and every living thing.*

CHAPTER 5

THE FIVE REIKI PRINCIPLES

The Reiki principles are spiritual ideals. By adopting these precepts you will add balance and substance to your life. It is important that you realise that you are not expected to live every moment of your life within the framework of these ideals. As humans we are all imperfect, and that is why each principle begins with "Just for today." You can without pressure or stress work on improving yourself daily. If you slip up today, you can always begin again tomorrow. The more you work with the principles, the more you will condition yourself to adopt them as a way of life.

To become more familiar with the Reiki principles it is advisable to read them aloud at least twice a day. You may wish to place a large copy of the ideals in a picture frame. Then you could position the copy in a prominent position where you are sure to see it each day, or if you are going to practise Reiki professionally, place it in your healing room. The Five Reiki principles mean different things to each one of us. Meditation will help to unlock your own perceptions. Simply sit or lie down in a comfortable position and close your eyes.

Repeat one of the ideals several times aloud using it as a mantra. As you drift into a meditative state become aware of what's happening inside your mind and body. You may experience many different feelings, emotions and thoughts. If you do this exercise in a group share your experiences and write down everything you've experienced. It is interesting to look at your notes on this exercise on a regular basis to see how you have grown by adopting these precepts. Repeat the exercise of meditating on each principle annually and compare notes or if in a group setting discuss the differences that have taken place.

JUST FOR TODAY I WILL NOT WORRY

Worry causes stress and anxiety leading to an imbalance of the mind body and spirit and blockage to the root chakra. The best way to overcome worry is to accept that all of us are faced with difficulties and setbacks in our lives. How we respond to them determines how we ultimately lead our lives. If you choose to respond negatively by getting upset and anxious towards one of life's setbacks you have chosen to damage the balance of your mind body and spirit. If you respond positively by accepting the setback as an opportunity to learn you can live a happier and more fulfilling life.

Allow yourself time each day to really laugh and have fun. Watch a funny movie or television show. Read a humorous book or magazine. Whatever it takes to make you laugh — do it. Ralph Waldo Emerson said, "Man surrounds himself with images of himself." This wonderful pearl of wisdom teaches us that if you want to be happy mix with happy people. Likewise if you want to be negative and constantly worrying you simple need to associate with people who are negative and worrisome.

Laughter is a wonderful healer. It has been proven through numerous studies that laughter can heal and in some cases prevent life threatening illnesses. Use this knowledge to live a healthier and longer life. Take responsibility for how you deal with life's setbacks. Have fun — life's too short to waste it worrying.

Use Reiki to re-balance your mind body and spirit and boost your resolve. Place one hand on the root chakra and the other hand on the heart chakra. Reiki will bring your mind body and spirit into equilibrium. Keep your hands over these chakra points for as long as you intuitively feel you need to. This Reiki technique will remove the blockages caused by stress, worry and anxiety. It can be used for self healing or on another person.

JUST FOR TODAY I WILL NOT BE ANGRY

Anger is an emotion. When we get angry we lose control of that emotion. In order to live by the above principle we must understand what triggers our anger and how we can choose to remove this destructive emotion from our being. In every confrontation that leads to anger the person or thing pushing your anger button has complete power and control over you. This simple realisation allows you to take back control of your emotions and as such you can now choose to respond to a situation in a positive way rather than react to a situation in a negative way.

Every time you meet someone there is an exchange of energy. If you are both happy and find the meeting was enjoyable then the energy exchange is neutral. However, if you lose control of your emotions and become angry, the other person steals your energy. Likewise, if someone gets angry at you then you are stealing their energy.

With this simple philosophy you can counter the endless situations or people that in the past have triggered your anger and caused you to react in an unhealthy manner. Next time someone honks their car horn at you or criticises you for no apparent reason smile and say to yourself I am not going to let you steal my energy.

Just imagine how much better you will feel when you choose not to react to negative people or situations. How many times in the past have you shouted abuse at another car driver and still felt the anger in your stomach an hour or so later. That person stole your energy. They probably drove on laughing at how silly you looked when you lost your composure. You allowed them to cause you stress, anger and probably indigestion. Only one person came out of this confrontation with their energy intact and it wasn't you.

Anger is a choice response. Decide each day not to allow your energy to be stolen from you by negative people or situations. On a physical level anger can cause stomach and digestive disorders. Choose to live a healthier life free from anger.

Use Reiki to assist the re-balancing process. Place one hand on the third eye chakra and the other hand on the root chakra. Keep your hands there for as long as you intuitively feel is necessary. This Reiki technique will help you control and eliminate this destructive emotion. It can be used for self healing or on another person.

JUST FOR TODAY I WILL DO MY WORK HONESTLY

Honesty means different things to different people. Many people feel it is fine to take home a few pens from the office, the company turn over millions in profit each year so they can afford to lose a few items of stationery. While another person will judge the same incident as an act of theft and believe that anyone found stealing stationery should be dismissed and charged with theft and even prosecuted.

Everyone at some point is dishonest. You may not steal from another person or company, but instead steal from yourself. For example if you a have a talent to help people and you choose not to then you are stealing from yourself by denying your gift.

You are also stealing from the people who could benefit from your talents.

Wasting your time on meaningless pursuits such as watching television for hours each day is stealing from your sacred and special time on Earth. Try to live your life to the best of your ability as honestly as you can. Honesty lives inside of you and doesn't care about being placed where others can view it. Finally, in your pursuit of a happier life I urge you to encapsulate the words from Michael Landon (the father in the television series "Little house on the Prairie") in his last interview before he died prematurely of cancer. He urged us to **"Live Every Second."**

Place one hand on the third eye chakra and the other hand on the solar plexus chakra to use Reiki to assist in the re-balancing of this principle. Keep your hands there for as long as you intuitively think they need to remain on these chakra points. This additional hand position can be used for healing yourself or other people.

Honesty is the best policy.
Richard Whately, Archbishop of Dublin

JUST FOR TODAY I WILL GIVE THANKS FOR MY MANY BLESSINGS.

Life tends to give us what we need, it may not be what we want but it will be what we need. Karmicly throughout our lives we receive what we need to grow and learn in this lifetime. If we grasp these lessons and grow accordingly we will become spiritually enlightened. Instead of wasting your life complaining of the things that have happened to you, and the problems you face. Step back for a moment on a regular basis and discover and appreciate the many blessings in your life.

Make a list of all your blessings. You will be amazed at how many wonderful things there are to give thanks for. Leave the materialistic things aside. They are shallow and meaningless. Pay attention to the things that are free and bring joy and humility to your life. Focus on the things in life that are free. For example, your mind, body, spirit, health, family, friends, flowers, trees, sea, sun, love, faith, knowledge, the countryside, animals, birds, etc., the list is endless.

When you appreciate the true wonders of life and let go of the materialistic things you are bound to enjoy your life more.

Place one hand on the third eye chakra and the other hand on the occipital ridge. Use Reiki to re-balance this principle in your life or in the life of another person.

JUST FOR TODAY I WILL BE KIND TO MY NEIGHBOUR AND EVERY LIVING THING.

The law of karma states that what goes around comes around. Send out love and you will receive love back in return. Send out kindness and you will receive kindness. Send out healing and you receive healing. Send out positive thoughts and you will receive positive results. Karma is a two edge sword. Send out negative thoughts and you will get negative results. Living within this precept will give you a happier and less stressful life full joy peace and love.

To bring balance to this principle for yourself or others first place one hand on the third eye chakra and the other hand on the root chakra. When you feel you are ready, move your hand from the third eye chakra to the throat chakra, and move your hand from the root chakra to the heart chakra keeping it there until you intuitively feel you have finished.

It is important to remember that the Reiki principles are only guides for a happier and more fulfilling life. Use meditation to unlock the true meaning of these precepts and incorporate them into your life. They will tranceform your life.

<u>They are not commandments, they are gifts of wisdom.</u>

CHAPTER 6

PREPARING FOR THE FIRST DEGREE

The Path To Reiki

People from all walks of life are drawn to Reiki for many different reasons. Many people come to Reiki after a personal recommendation from a friend who has already attended a workshop. They notice positive changes in their friend and decide to experience it for themselves. A large majority of people simply need healing and want to take responsibility and control of their own treatment and well-being. The most common factor seems to be that people are searching for hope and guidance. Often people feel empty and are looking for a way of filling that void.

Many students begin as sceptics just curious to find out more about it, and leave as Reiki enthusiasts. The secret to getting the most from Reiki is to be open to Reiki. Instead of being negative and sceptical let the joy of Reiki envelop you. Leave your fears and doubts behind and jump head first in to a life changing experience. Reiki draws you to itself. If you are attending a seminar / workshop on first degree Reiki, you are their for a reason — **you need it.** Trust in the omniscient wisdom of Reiki. Remember you will only need the First Degree attunements once in your life, so make it a celebration you will never forget. *It's up to you.*

The Initiation Ceremony

In order to work with, and become a channel for Reiki you need to go through the first degree initiation ceremony, which consists of four attunements. These attunements are normally done over the course of a two day workshop. I prefer to do the four attunements at the same time as I believe it is beneficial to the student. The energy is stronger and the student is able to work and practice at their full capacity throughout the workshop. This process also allows the student to feel, sense and experience more of the Reiki energy.

The four attunements are given on both days of the workshop, to supercharge the student and raise their energy vibration to the peak level possible with first degree Reiki.

Preparing For The Workshop

Before attending the first degree workshop there are a few basic things you should do in preparation. These guidelines will enable you to get the most from the workshop and the Initiation ceremony.

♦ Avoid taking alcohol or any other form of drug for at least forty-eight hours before the workshop. These substances slow and hinder the flow of Reiki throughout the body.

♦ Avoid eating meat, fish, processed foods or any other junk food for at least twenty-four hours. If possible have a day of fresh fruit, salad and vegetables. The digestion of food takes more energy than any other bodily function. Proteins and highly processed foods take more time to digest and will steal vital energy from your body.

♦ If possible meditate each day for a week before attending the workshop. This will help to focus your thoughts, expectations and mind on becoming a Reiki channel for healing.

The Morning Of The Workshop

♦ Get up earlier than normal so you have plenty of time to prepare for the day ahead. You will then have time to relax and not become rushed or stressed.

♦ If possible take a walk or a gentle jog to energise your system.

♦ Avoid tea or coffee. However, naturally caffeine free herbal tea is fine.

♦ Eat only fruit for breakfast. You will have more energy for the workshop.

♦ Mentally prepare yourself with a short meditation.

♦ Give yourself plenty of time to reach your destination. The stress of being late can upset your day and your enjoyment.

♦ Come to the workshop with an open mind body and spirit. You will get out only what you put into the workshop.

What Happens During The Initiation?

Many people wonder why the initiation ceremony must remain a secret and why the students need to close their eyes during the attunements. Questions like these are quite normal, and understandable. The reason for the secrecy is to keep the rituals sacred and cherished by the Reiki Master and their students. The eyes kept closed allow the recipient being attuned to go inside and focus on the experience, it also helps the Reiki Master concentrate on what is a complex set of procedures.

During the initiation, the Reiki Master uses the ancient symbols and mantras (holy words that activate and direct certain energies) rediscovered by Dr. Usui to connect the student to the universal life force.

Dr. Hayashi described it to Madam Takata so beautifully when he said, "the universal life force is so big we cannot measure it, so deep we cannot fathom it; therefore in Japanese we call it Reiki." He continued "it is comparable to a radio station, broadcasting radio waves everywhere. There are no wires connecting the radio station with your home, yet when you turn on the receiver and tune into the radio waves from the station you receive what they are sending. Likewise, the principles of Reiki are the same. The energy is everywhere, it travels through space without wires. Once you have been connected to the energy it flows automatically, forever. It is a universal and immeasurable energy and its power is unlimited."

What Happens After Initiation?

When you receive your first attunement during the initiation ceremony, energy will start to flow through your hands at the thought of healing. You will also start a 21 day cleansing and detoxification cycle through the chakras. The Reiki attunement has a powerful healing influence on the mind body and spirit, activating all seven chakras, beginning with the root, and ending at the crown chakra — each one taking approximately twenty-four hours. This happens three times.

You may not be aware of this depending on how fit and healthy you are. The more toxic you are the more you will be aware of the cleansing process. Your body is preparing you for healing. When the toxins are out of your system your body can work at its ultimate level for healing. Your whole system will be readjusted and re-balanced. You may experience symptoms of physical cleansing and detoxification such as a running nose, headaches or diarrhoea. There is no need to be alarmed the body is simply flushing out the toxins. It is a good idea to spend a bit more time resting over the twenty-one day period. Use the time for self healing and reflection. Place your hands on any aches or pains you may be experiencing and allow Reiki to ease your discomfort and speed up the healing process.

The healing energy works on all levels of the mind body and spirit. This process can be quite emotional and exhausting at times as the Reiki energy goes to work on the emotional and physical blocks, scars and baggage that your body has collected and stored throughout your lifetime.

Reiki's wisdom will do whatever is needed to release your from the fears and barriers that prevent you leading a happy fulfilling life. If you find yourself getting emotional and wanting to cry, scream or shout, let it happen. The old saying *better out than in* is so true and therapeutically beneficial to your being. Release the ties that bind you to your old habits and lifestyle. Reiki is like a rebirth. You can cleanse your mind body and spirit and start again. Trust in the healing power of Reiki.

Some reactions may seem unpleasant but by accepting them as part of your personal healing process and not attaching a great deal of importance to them, they will soon pass. You may also find yourself dealing with certain issues in your dreams, it can be helpful to keep a record of them in a dream journal. Then when you have time you can meditate on the issues. There are also two extremely good techniques for unravelling the meanings of dreams and how they relate to your life.

The first is 'Dreamwork' which is a form of Gestalt therapy developed by Dr Fritz Perls. It is simple and easy to understand. You are shown how to conduct conversations with your dreams. During these conversations your unconscious mind will unlock and reveal the true meaning of your dreams to you. There are many good books on this subject including *The Red Book of Gestalt* by Gaie Houston.

Professor Eugene Gendlin developed another technique for working with your dreams called Focussing. This subtle yet profound skill teaches you how to get in touch with the wisdom of the body. Ann Weiser Cornell's excellent book *The Power of Focusing* is a practical guide to using Professor Gendlin's techniques to unravel the meanings of your dreams.

The attunements 'switch on' an extra surge of power which fuels all life. The more you use Reiki the stronger it becomes. Establish the habit of giving yourself Reiki before you fall asleep at night and when you wake up in the morning. Remember, once you have been attuned to the universal life force you can begin channelling the healing energy of Reiki to yourself and others.

Reiki is never sent, it is always drawn through the channel. This is one of the major differences between Reiki and magnetic or spiritual healing. Because the energy is drawn through the channel by the recipient as opposed to being directed by the healer, the Reiki practitioner will never feel drained or take on the condition of the patient. On the contrary, the practitioner is also receiving a self - treatment as the Reiki energy flows through them to the recipient.

Your psychic, intuitive and creative abilities will be raised by between 50 to 80 percent. By raising your vibratory level you will begin a *Tranceformational* process on all the many levels and aspects of your life.

We all live in an extremely stressful and hectic world, which can influence our total being. Reiki helps control how our mind body and spirit responds both internally and externally to the often negative and destructive external stimuli from our world. If applied regularly, Reiki will reduce the extreme highs and lows of life, gradually leading to a new balanced existence.

Ways To Use Reiki After The Attunement

Once you have been attuned to Reiki, the energy will flow through your hands whenever you touch with the intention of healing or helping. *You can use Reiki on:*

☯ Yourself	☯ Plants	☯ Letters
☯ Other Adults	☯ Trees	☯ Documents
☯ children	☯ Seeds	☯ Your car
☯ Prenatal babies	☯ Crystals	☯ For protection
☯ Accidents	☯ Food	☯ Travelling
☯ Emergencies	☯ Drinks	☯ Your home
☯ Animals	☯ Your work	☯ Drinking water
☯ Birds	☯ Contracts	☯ Bath water
☯ Fish	☯ Projects	☯ Shower water

The list is endless, you are only limited by your imagination!

CHAPTER 7

ANATOMIC ILLUSTRATIONS

Reiki with its infinite wisdom goes to the place in the body that requires healing. That is why Reiki is so easy to learn and apply. There is no need to study the anatomy of the human body or animals to treat a person or animal successfully. You simply place your hands on the body and channel the energy. Reiki will do the rest.

However, it can be helpful to know where the major organs, lymphatic and endocrine systems are in the body. This knowledge will allow you to treat specific problems or organs quickly and easily.

The following illustrations are simple diagrams of the human anatomy. If you decide to further your studies we recommend that you make full use of your public library. They will have books on the Human anatomy as well as books on the anatomy of various pets and animals. If you have a PC we can recommend Bodyworks, an excellent guide to the anatomy.

THE ENDOCRINE SYSTEM

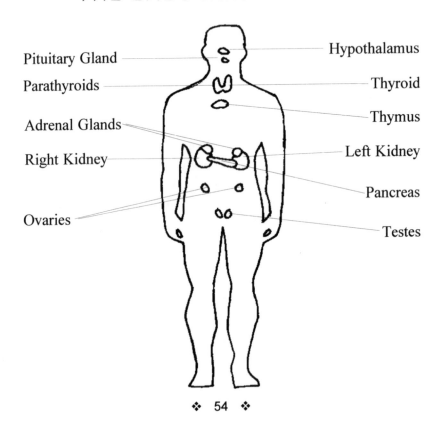

Pituitary Gland

Parathyroids

Adrenal Glands

Right Kidney

Ovaries

Hypothalamus

Thyroid

Thymus

Left Kidney

Pancreas

Testes

THE MAJOR BODY ORGANS

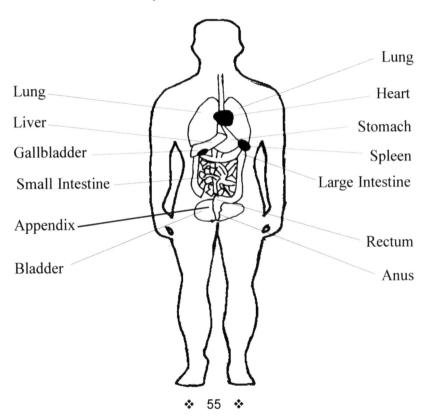

THE LYMPHATIC SYSTEM

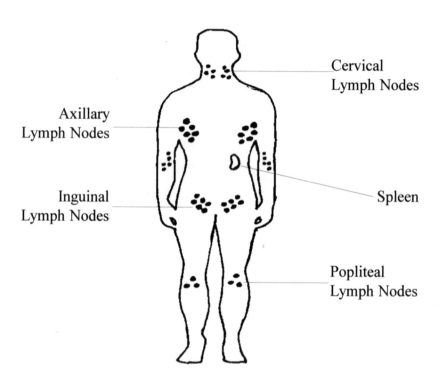

Cervical
Lymph Nodes

Axillary
Lymph Nodes

Inguinal
Lymph Nodes

Spleen

Popliteal
Lymph Nodes

CHAPTER 8

SELF TREATMENT

Once you have received the first degree attunements, from a Reiki Master you are ready to work with the universal life force. However, it is important that you realise as with every profession there is a need to first practice and master the skills associated with healing. Madam Takata taught her students to heal themselves first, then their families, then their friends. Only then did she believe they would be adequately qualified and able to work as a practitioner and heal other people.

When a person first learns to drive a car they need time, practice and experience to master what appears to be a rather complex set of procedures. However, within a relatively short space of time they can drive safely and effortlessly as they unconsciously control the car and all the various skills associated with driving. Likewise with time practice and experience you will master the skills and techniques associated with art of

Reiki healing. Treat the early months as a learning experience, almost like an apprenticeship, this will give you the time you need to develop your confidence and skills. Remember the more you work with Reiki the more intuitive you will become, your vibrations will be raised and you will develop and experience a new joyful consistency in your life.

Self healing is the starting point for personal development and self discovery. Reiki is not just a tool for healing, it also brings protection, prevention and personal transformation on all levels. As you progress along your new path, inevitably you will come up against obstacles and setbacks in your life that often seem like the whole ocean front, but with Reiki you will have the strength to deal with them as though they are but pebbles on the beach. Even if you never use Reiki to heal anyone but yourself, you will find a new sense of balance and peace in your life.

There is no other method of self-treatment as simple and as effective as Reiki. Because Reiki is always available to you, whenever you feel tired, stressed, have any aches or pains, you can alleviate them by simply laying your hands on your body. The infinite wisdom of Reiki will go to wherever it is needed.

Recharge your batteries every day, not just when problems, difficulties, anxiety or illnesses arise. Daily self treatment will prevent sickness and disease, and bring your life into focus and balance quickly. Every time you use Reiki on yourself, you raise your self esteem and self love. You will discover your mission in life and become more compassionate and loving.

Instead of getting stressed at the normal things you come into contact with each day such as traffic jams, meetings, interviews, going to the doctor's or dentist, waiting in queues, your children needs and your family responsibilities to name but a few, allow Reiki into your life and let Reiki become a new way of life to you.

Set aside a little time each day for a self treatment. First thing in the morning will give you a positive boost for the day ahead. Alternatively, a self treatment last thing at night will relax and unwind you, leading to a good nights sleep. Good places for a self-treatment are in the bath, the shower, or lying in bed. The possibilities are endless and the benefits are immeasurable.

Reiki is a gift to be savoured and enjoyed. Remember the more you use Reiki the stronger and more profound it becomes. Daily use could extend your own life by a number of years.

HOW REIKI CAN HELP YOU

Using Reiki on a daily basis for self-treatment, you will find the following benefits occur without any effort.

- ☯ Reiki will relax you when you are stressed.
- ☯ Reiki brings about deep relaxation.
- ☯ Reiki Centres your thoughts when you are confused.
- ☯ Reiki energises you when you feel drained.
- ☯ Reiki calms you when you are frightened.
- ☯ Reiki focuses your mind and helps you to solve problems.
- ☯ Reiki relieves pain.
- ☯ Reiki accelerates natural healing of wounds.
- ☯ Reiki improves health.
- ☯ Reiki gradually clears up chronic problems.
- ☯ Reiki prevents the development of disease.
- ☯ Reiki detoxifies the body.
- ☯ Reiki dissolves energy blockages.
- ☯ Reiki releases emotional wounds.
- ☯ Reiki increases the vibrational frequency of the body.
- ☯ Reiki helps change negative conditioning & behaviour.

HOW TO TREAT YOURSELF WITH REIKI

There is no right or wrong way to work with Reiki on oneself. As you become more experienced with the Reiki energy you will intuitively move your hands to wherever it feels right. However, if you are aware of a specific problem such as an injury or pain, then you should place your hands directly over that area to begin with , and follow up with a full self treatment. In the beginning, it is always best to follow a set procedure as shown in the following illustrations marked "Self Treatment Hand Positions".

When you have mastered the hand positions you can then leave each self treatment up to your own intuition. You may wish to worked with music to add the right relaxing mood. Find a place where you won't be disturbed if possible. Normally you would spend three to five minutes on each position. However, time is often short, but remember a little Reiki is better than no

Reiki. On completion of the self treatment drink a large glass of purified water. Close your eyes and go inside and pay attention to the thoughts and emotions that have arisen during the session. You may feel light headed, and if you need to rest, or sit down for a short time, allow yourself this time.

If you feel you need to continue to work on a specific area of the body, even if you have completed a full self treatment, then go with your intuition, always listen to your mind and body.

Remember the following hand positions are only a guide use your intuition

---

SELF HEALING HAND POSITIONS
Position 1

- Cup your hands and gently rest them over your eyes, cheekbones and forehead (third eye chakra).
- Stress, eye problems, asthma, head colds, allergies, sinuses, pituitary gland, pineal gland, cerebral nerves.

SELF HEALING HAND POSITIONS

<u>Position 2</u>

- ◆ Place your hands on the top of your head fingertips touching (crown chakra).
- ◆ Migraine, headaches, eye problems, multiple sclerosis, stress, bladder, digestive disorders, flatulence, emotional problems.

<u>Position 3</u>

- ◆ Hands on either side of your head with fingers covering your temples.
- ◆ Balance, tinnitus, hearing & ear problems, colds, flu, balances the functions of the right & left brain.

SELF HEALING HAND POSITIONS

Position 4

- ◆ Place your hands on the back of your head covering the occipital ridge.
- ◆ Headaches, eye problems, stress, hay fever, sinuses, digestive disorders, fears, phobias, shock, depression, stroke.

Position 5

- ◆ Hands covering the top of the shoulders and the bottom of the neck.
- ◆ Aches & pains, stress, neck, tight muscles, nerves, spinal injuries and shock.

SELF HEALING HAND POSITIONS

Position 6

- Place your hands around the neck with the heels covering the throat (throat chakra).
- Self expression, communication, breathing, voice and speech problems, bronchitis, flu, colds, anger.

Position 7

- Hands form a T, left hand covering the heart (heart chakra) and the right hand over the thymus gland.
- Heart, angina,lungs, thymus, thyroid, weight problems, immune system, lymph, emotional problems, stress,

SELF HEALING HAND POSITIONS

Position 8-11

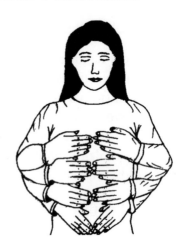

♦ Hands are positioned horizontally at the top of the torso with fingertips touching. Move hands down as shown until finally ending in a V inside the hip bone.

♦ All major organs and glands, disease, infections, stomach, intestines, reproductive system, anger, emotions.

Position 12

♦ Place hands over the front and back of right knee.

♦ Leg pains, varicose veins.

Position 13

♦ Place hands over the front and back of left knee.

♦ Leg pains, varicose veins.

SELF HEALING HAND POSITIONS

Position 14-17

♦ Hands are positioned horizontally at the top of the back with fingertips touching. Move hands down as shown until finally ending at the base of the spine.

♦ All major organs and glands, disease, infections, back and spinal problems, stress,

Position 18

♦ Place hands on the top and underside of right foot.

♦ Leg pains, varicose veins, all major organs and glands (reflexology points).

Position 19

♦ Place hands on the top and underside of left foot.

♦ Leg pains, varicose veins, all major organs and glands (reflexology points).

The cure for pain is in the pain.
Roger Woolger

CHAPTER 9

PREPARING TO TREAT OTHERS

Appropriate Environment

It is important to create the right setting whenever possible for a Reiki healing session. You may work from home and be able to use a spare room just for healing. If this is not practical you may want to look at the viability of joining a local therapy centre that offer healing rooms at a reasonable price.

The room should be light and clean, and feel safe. Bright pastel colours such as white, yellow or purple can be used to create the desired effect. Make sure you will not be interrupted by internal or external distractions, so unplug the telephone and disconnect the doorbell. If your working from home let your family or friends know your schedules so they do not disturb you.

If possible always use a therapy table. Alternatively, you could use a strong table with thick blankets on top. You will need two pillows, one for the clients head and other for their feet. Make sure the room is heated to a comfortable level. Some people may get cold just lying still on your treatment table so always have a warm blanket available.

Add a plant to the room and some crystals under the table to help with the right energy. Some people like to work in total silence during a session. Personally we prefer to always work with therapeutic music such as classical, ambient or new age to help our clients relax. Music also can help the therapist relax and allow them to focus on healing. Natural sounds such as whales, dolphins and running water are very therapeutic and relaxing.

The *Free CD Heartbeat* enclosed with this book is extremely relaxing and therapeutic. We recommend you play this music while you treat other people and yourself with Reiki. There are also a wide range of compact discs and tapes available that have been created specifically for Reiki. They have been designed to run for the length of a full treatment with a bell or chime added at three or five minute intervals to let the therapist know when to move their hands to another position.

Burning incense or oils can add a pleasing aroma to your room. However, be careful as some people are sensitive to certain smells and it may cause them to have an unpleasant therapy session. To prevent this happening ask your client before you light your oils or incense sticks. During a Reiki session you may find your client begins to cry as they release blocked emotional issues, so always keep a box of tissues handy for these occasions.

For a finishing touch to your room you may want to place photographs of Dr. Usui, Dr. Hayashi, Madam Takata, Jesus or Sai Baba, depending on who you call upon during your invocation / prayer.

Remove All Jewellery

Reiki can travel through all materials such as stone, brick, concrete and metal. However, the metal and stones used in the manufacture of jewellery come into contact with and attract certain types of negative energy. To enable you to work with Reiki free from all subtle energy disturbances it is advisable to remove all jewellery such as rings, watches, earrings, chains and necklaces.

Therapist who work with precious stones and crystals for healing recognise that these materials can become saturated with negative energy. That is why they cleanse them on a regular basis.

Remove Tight Clothing

To allow Reiki to flow freely through you and your client it is important that you both remove tight clothing such as belts, ties and shoes. This will also make you feel more comfortable and relaxed. Reiki can travel through clothes so there is no need to remove any other forms of clothing. You may find it more comfortable if you wear loose fighting clothes when you are working with Reiki such as a tracksuit.

Avoid Alcohol

Alcohol dissipates energy. Always refrain from consuming alcohol if you know you are going to be working with Reiki for at least twenty-four hours before a session.

Personal Hygiene

Ensure you smell and appear clean and fresh. Avoid wearing strong perfumes or after shaves. If you smoke make sure you brush you teeth or use a mouth freshener. Refrain from eating garlic, onions or any other food that may leave a smell on your breath. Wash your hands before a Reiki session using a lightly scented or neutral soap. Your hands come into contact with your clients face and skin so it is important for hygiene purposes and the peace of mind of your client to have clean hands.

We personally always use Vibhooti. The sacred ash that materialises from the hands of Sai Baba. We feel it brings us closer to Sri Sathya Sai Baba who is an Avatar and holy man. Rubbing Vibhooti into the palms of the hands creates an increase in energy and a connection with Sai Baba. The different is profound. The scent of the Vibhooti is also extremely relaxing and sweet smelling making your hands smell wonderful. Our clients always comment on the beautiful smell and ask where it is coming from. For more information about Sai Baba or Vibhooti contact The Sathya Sai Book Centre 19 Hay Lane, Kingsbury London NW9 0NH. Tel (44) 0181 732 2886 or e-mail: saibooks@fastaccess.co.uk they stock a large selection of books, videos and Vibhooti.

"Come, test, inquire, taste, experience."

Sai Baba

The Invocation

It is important to remember that as a Reiki practitioner you are not healing your clients. The people receiving Reiki are in fact healing themselves. You are merely the channel that enables them to draw the Reiki energy through your hands to the place it is needed. The invocation is a token that symbolises you are giving up any claims to power. You are simply the conduit in which the infinite power of the universal life force flows.

Although the invocation is not necessary to turn on the Reiki energy I feel it enables the therapist to disassociate themselves from their ego and pay respect to the universal life force and the person they are about to work with.

Your prayer should be personal and in line with your own beliefs. Ask for permission to be used as a channel for Reiki healing. On the following page is our own personal invocation which may help you develop a prayer that is suitable for your own use.

Once your client is relaxed and ready to receive Reiki stand behind them and close your eyes. If appropriate rub Vibhooti into your hands and join them together in a prayer like position in front of your heart chakra. Alternatively, if your client is seated, place your hands on their shoulders for the invocation.

Garry & Adele Malone's Personal Invocation

We always like to take a few moments before we begin a treatment to mentally prepare ourselves for working as a channel for Reiki. This quiet time is perfect for getting in touch with our guides, mentors and assistants. It allows us a brief moment of reflection and focusses our thoughts on healing. It is important to begin the treatment with the right mental attitude. Your wish should be to pass on unconditional love and healing in the purest form and sense.

"I call upon my lord God the absolute power, his son Jesus Christ, all the Saints and Angelic beings who have work with Reiki in the past especially Dr. Usui, Dr. Hayashi, Madam Takata and all the Reiki Masters past, present and future. I call upon Sai Baba, Mother Meera, my guides and my sister Kim Buckley to draw near and take part in this healing session. Allow me to become a channel for your unconditional love and

healing on behalf of_____ (insert clients name) may Reiki's infinite wisdom go exactly where it is needed most, should it be for their higher good. May we all be empowered by your divine love and blessing? Amen.

Cleanse And Harmonise Your Clients Aura

Prior to commencing the Reiki treatment run your hands in your clients aura about six inches above their body from their head right down to their feet in a slow smooth motion at least three times to remove any superficial energy build ups. This will also bring harmony to your clients aura and form a positive rapport between you and your client. Pay attention to your hands, use your intuition, sense for possible blockages or hot spots to focus on during your healing session. You are now ready to begin the treatment.

If ye have faith as a grain of mustard seed,
ye shall say unto this mountain,
Remove hence to yonder place; and it shall remove

St. Matthew 17:20

CHAPTER 10

TREATING OTHERS

Before you begin a full body treatment on another person there are a few important points to remember.

♦ Never give a Reiki treatment to a person who has a pacemaker as Reiki can alter its rhythm.

♦ Never give a Reiki treatment to a person who suffers from Diabetes Mellitus and are taking insulin injections, unless they are prepared to check their insulin levels every day as Reiki reduces the amount of insulin they require.

♦ Always explain to a person who is visiting you for the first time for a Reiki treatment exactly what you are going to do and the type of reactions that might occur. Stress that any one of these reactions are normal. They may experience one or two of these reactions, all of them or none of them. It makes no difference. Reiki will go wherever it is needed.

The type of reactions that may occur are:

- A sensation of heat
- A sensation of cold
- See colours
- Past life flashes
- Involuntary movements
- Fall asleep

- Itchiness
- Emotional responses
- Rumbling stomach
- memory flashes
- pins and needles
- sense your hands moving

- Often the client will experience extreme cold at the position of your hands while you feel intense heat.

- If the client experiences nothing explain to them that the Reiki energy often works on a subtle level yet has profound results which normally become apparent in the following days or weeks.

- Never forget the client is drawing Reiki through you. They are doing the healing on a subconscious level. You are only the channel.

- Reiki always travels to the place it is needed most.

◆ No knowledge of the human anatomy or physiology is required to work with Reiki. Leave your ego aside and Reiki will do the work.

◆ Forget the symptoms treat the whole person.

◆ Listen to your clients body through your hands. Sense the different types of energy. If the energy is strong keep your hands in that position until your sense a shift in the energy level. Use your intuition.

◆ Look for non-verbal communication from your clients body. Deep sighs or hand and leg movements indicate something positive is taking place.

◆ The normal time required for a full body treatment is between sixty to ninety minutes.

◆ At the end of a treatment always offer your client a glass of cold water to aid grounding. Always wash your hands under cold running water after each treatment.

Beginning The Treatment

♦ Ensure your client is lying flat on the therapy table with their arms down by their sides. Their legs should also be flat against the table and must not be crossed as this may block the flow of Reiki.

♦ Gently lay your hands on your clients body. Keep them in each position for between three to five minutes. As you become more experienced use your intuition.

♦ Your hands should be cupped with your fingers firmly closed as though you were trying to hold water. This keeps the channel strong between your client and the universal life force. If your fingers are open Reiki can escape just as water would slip through your open fingers.

♦ In the case of burnt skin or a clients genitals and breasts hold your hands just above their body.

♦ **Don't forget the box of tissues.**

FULL BODY TREATMENT - HAND POSITIONS

> **Remember the following hand positions are only a guide use your intuition**

Position 1

- Cup your hands and gently rest them over your clients eyes, cheekbones and forehead (third eye chakra).
- Stress, eye problems, asthma, head colds, allergies, sinuses, pituitary gland, pineal gland, cerebral nerves.

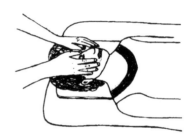

Position 2

- Place your hands on the top of your clients head with palms covering the crown chakra.
- Migraine, headaches, eye problems, multiple sclerosis, stress, bladder, digestive disorders, flatulence, emotional problems.

FULL BODY TREATMENT - HAND POSITIONS

Position 3

- Hands on either side of your clients head with palms covering their temples.
- Balance, tinnitus, hearing & ear problems, colds, flu, balances the functions of the right & left brain.

Position 4

- Move your hands to the back of your clients head covering their occipital ridge.
- Headaches, eye problems, stress, hay fever, sinuses, digestive disorders, fears, phobias, shock, depression, stroke.

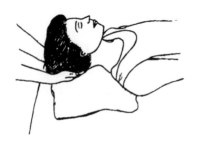

FULL BODY TREATMENT - HAND POSITIONS

Position 5

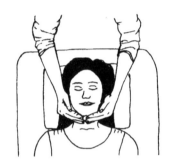

- Place your hands along your clients jawbones covering the throat chakra.
- Self expression, communication, breathing, voice and speech problems, bronchitis, flu, colds, anger.

Position 6

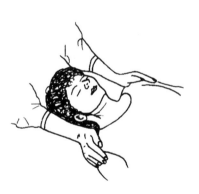

- Place your hands on your clients shoulders.
- Aches and Pain in the arms elbows and hands, tight shoulder muscles, Stress, cold hands, disrupted blood supply to the arms and hands.

FULL BODY TREATMENT - HAND POSITIONS

<u>Position 7-12</u>

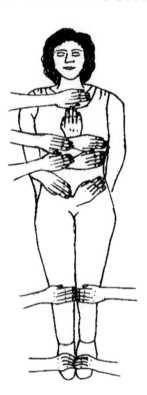

◆ Begin by forming a T, covering the heart chakra and the collarbone. Then move your hands down and across the torso covering the solar plexus and sacral chakras. Form a V, to cover the root chakra. Finally place your hands over your clients knees and feet.

◆ All major organs and glands, disease, infections, stomach, intestines, reproductive system, anger, stress, emotions, leg pains, varicose veins.

FULL BODY TREATMENT - HAND POSITIONS

Position 13-20

- Begin by placing your hands across your clients shoulder blades. Move hands down as shown until your reach the base of the spine. Form a T, as shown covering the Root chakra. Finally place your hands across the back of your clients knees and the undersides of their feet.

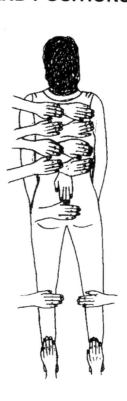

- All major organs and glands, disease, infections, stomach, intestines, back and spinal problems, reproductive system, anger, stress, emotions, leg pains, varicose veins. Treat all major organs and glands through the reflexology points on the feet.

Finally

♦ When all the positions have been treated, place your left hand on your clients crown chakra and your right hand at the base of their spine. This final position balances the energy in your clients body.

♦ Complete your treatment by combing your clients aura. Stroke the body firmly from the crown down to the feet in a sweeping motion. Continue past the feet until you touch the floor for grounding. Repeat for a second time lightly touching the body. Finally comb the aura a few inches above the body.

CHAPTER 11

AN ALTERNATIVE REIKI TREATMENT

Rapid Reiki

On many occasions you will find it's not practical to spend sixty to ninety minutes conducting a complete Reiki treatment. Often for numerous reasons the person needing Reiki has a limited amount of time or you simply are called into action in a place far away from your normal healing room. There is an alternative quick and versatile technique that can be used in these situations. The Rapid Reiki treatment focusses on all the major chakra points while the client sits upright in a chair, and takes between thirty to forty-five minutes to complete.

The Rapid Reiki Treatment

♦ **1st Position:** (Your client should be seated) Stand behind your client. Place your hands on your client's shoulders. Silently make your own personal invocation.

- **2nd Position**: Remain behind your client. Place both hands on the top of your clients head covering the crown chakra.

- **3rd Position**: Move to the side of your client. Place one hand on their forehead at the third eye chakra and the other hand over the occipital ridge at the back of their head.

- **4th Position**: Remain at the side of your client. Place one hand over the throat chakra at the centre of your clients neck and the other hand parallel on the back of their neck.

- **5th Position:** Remain at the side of your client. Place one hand on their heart chakra at the centre of their chest and the other hand parallel between your clients shoulder blades.

- **6th Position**: Remain at the side of your client. Place one hand on the solar plexus and the other hand parallel on the clients spine.

♦   **7th Position:** Remain at the side of your client. Place one hand on the base of your clients stomach covering the sacral chakra and the other hand parallel on the base of your clients spine.

♦   **8th Position**: Move round to the front of your client and place one hand on each knee.

♦   **9th Position**: Kneel down in front of your client and place one hand over each of your clients feet with thumbs open, cupping feet to floor.

Finally comb your clients aura three times as you normally would after a full treatment. Wash your hands in cold running water and offer a cold drink of water to your client to assist grounding.

Please Note: For your comfort positions 3 - 8 should be conducted while sitting in a chair. Spend 3 - 5 minutes on each position unless your intuition tells you otherwise.

A little Reiki is better than no Reiki at all.

CHAPTER 12

THE ULTRADIAN RHYTHM TECHNIQUE

What is The Ultradian Rhythm

Biological research has discovered that the human body functions in various cycles. One of these cycles is the ultradian rhythm — the natural body cycle of activity and rest. During sleep we dream every 90-120 minutes, even if we don't always remember doing so. In our daily lives this rhythm continues.

During the day we often have a sudden urge to stop and rest. The body needs to take short breaks every 90-120 minutes to repair and maintain itself. Most people misjudge this natural and important process and fail to allow themselves a short power break. Instead of relaxing and recharging their batteries most people opt for a quick boost of power. This normally comes in the form of a coffee or tea break, sweets, chocolates, fizzy drinks or cigarettes. Unfortunately all these are stimulants and simple gloss over the underlying need of the body to take regular breaks if it is to maintain health and well-being. When we consistently ignore these essential psycho-physiological breaks we are upsetting the fine balance and rhythms of the mind body and spirit.

This neglect leads to health problems and stress-related disorders such as depression, mood disorders, psychosomatic pain and illnesses, sexual dysfunction, eating disorders and a wide variety of psychological problems. Reiki can be used to prevent and help treat this problem by bringing the body back into equilibrium and normalising the ultradian rhythm.

The Ultradian Rhythm Technique

During the day look out for signs from your bodymind telling you to stop for a moment and rest. These signs normally manifest as a sudden feeling of slowing down or loss of energy. You may feel yourself drift off into a semi-trance like state, somewhat like daydreaming.

At this point allow yourself a short break and you will revitalise and rejuvenate your whole mind body and spirit. Place your cupped hands over your eyes as shown on page 62 (self healing hand positions). Close your eyes and go inside. Become aware of any part of the body that feels tight, sore or tired. If you discover a part of your body that needs Reiki move your hands to that place and keep them there for as long as you need to. Try to imagine or sense that part of your body being filled with a healing light - Reiki.

Then make the light grow brighter and brighter, larger and larger until it envelops your whole body. Sense the feeling of peace and well-being as the healing light fills your aura and forms a protective shield of pure unconditional love and energy around you. When you feel rejuvenated and recharged gently open your eyes and continue with your day.

Repeat this exercise on a regular basis to keep your energy levels high and prevent stress and ill health. It is important to change how you respond to this natural rhythm. Replace the junk food and quick attempts to boost your energy levels with this healthier and natural self healing technique that will add years to your life.

If you fail to find a part of the body that needs Reiki. Go back inside once more and look again. Often we have found it takes a second look to find a part of the body that requires healing. This is because it is invariably hidden deep in the unconscious mind. However, if you fail to uncover anything simply keep your hands over your eyes for as long as you require. This short break will still be beneficial to your health and well-being.

When time or conditions prevent you taking these short power breaks, there is another simple way of maintaining your fight against sickness and disease. The thymus gland which is situated between the throat and heart chakra (see page 54) is a twin lobed organ that is responsible for producing white infection-fighting blood cells. Although the functions of the thymus are not fully understood, it is known to play an important part in developing immunities against various diseases by forming a hormone essential to the immune system known as THF (thymic humoral factor). Researchers believe that it is this hormone that acts on lymphocytes, causing them to change into plasma cells, which subsequently form antibodies that produce immunities.

Tap gently 20-30 times on your chest over the position of the thymus or place one of your hands over this position for several minutes. This simple technique will help maintain and boost your immune system while filling your body with vitality.

CHAPTER 13

GROUP TREATMENT

Group treatments were first used by Dr Hayashi at his clinic in Tokyo. He would often treat clients with the help of several other Reiki practitioners. Many people find it more enjoyable to work with another person or persons. There are of course several advantages to working in a group.

The Benefits of Group Treatment.

- Group Treatment is quicker taking as little as six to ten minutes to complete a full Reiki treatment.
- Group Treatment is very powerful. The client receives an intense burst of healing energy. This often has the effect of kick starting the clients natural healing process.
- Group Treatment allows the team to form a bond and create a unique energy. As we all experience Reiki in different ways, clients will often notice the different energy vibrations from different Reiki practitioners.

Guidelines For Conducting A Group Treatment

♦ All the normal preparations and procedures of a full Reiki treatment still apply to a group session.

♦ Before you begin a group treatment decide who will work on the head positions and ultimately control the healing session.

♦ Depending on how many Reiki practitioners are involved in the group treatment decide who will work on the various hand positions. Don't forget to decide who will complete the session by smoothing the clients aura.

♦ If four or more practitioners are taking part in the healing session you can have one practitioner at each end of the clients body while the other practitioners work in the middle.

♦ Remember to have a box of tissues available.

♦ This is a wonderful way to treat many people in a short space of time and ideal for therapy days. However, remember to wash your hands before and after each treatment under cold running water to dissipate any negative energy and assist grounding for each member of the team.

♦ Spend time sharing experiences. Group treatment is a great way to learn and grow together.

CHAPTER 14

PREGNANCY - BABIES - CHILDREN

Pregnancy

Reiki is both safe and extremely beneficial to an unborn child and their pregnant mother. We have found that women who have studied the first degree and are attuned to the universal life force find the experience of pregnancy and childbirth more enjoyable and easier to cope with. Reiki can help during pregnancy in various ways such as:

♦ Reiki alleviates morning sickness.
♦ Reiki reducing stress and tiredness.
♦ Reiki stimulates the babies healthy development.
♦ Reiki can be used to treat painful muscles, joints or the spine.
♦ Reiki strengthens the bond between a mother and her baby. When a mother who is attuned to Reiki places her hands on her tummy she is passing pure unconditional love and healing to her unborn child.

- Reiki keeps the mind body and spirit in balance reducing the chances of post natal depression.
- Reiki nourishes the foetus with love and the universal life force. It gently comforts, protects and envelops the unborn baby.

Note: If the father of an unborn baby is a Reiki practitioner he can also help during the pregnancy by treating his partner. The important bond between father and child will also be stimulated each time he places his hands on his partners pregnant tummy. The father can communicate through his hands with his child.

Further Note: Reiki can help couples who are finding it difficult to conceive a child by reducing stress and stimulating both the females natural reproductive cycle and the males production of sperm. In many cases when a couple are desperate for a child they place extreme stress on themselves causing an imbalance of their mind body and spirits. So often the moment they give up and forget about trying to have children, and the pressure and stress factor is removed many couples find their prayers are answered and a pregnancy is discovered.

Babies

♦ Reiki can hasten the recovery time of the mother and baby after the birth. It is particularly good for caesarians sections and healing the various scars and stitches often associated with childbirth.
♦ Reiki can be used to heal a new born baby's umbilical cord.
♦ Reiki can be used to vitalise and nourish the mothers milk if the baby is breast feed. Alternatively, if the baby is to be bottle feed the formula can be treated with Reiki. Treating and enriching the babies food can help nourish and satisfy the babies hunger. This will help them suckle until they are content and full. Regular filling feeds lead to less sleepless nights. Something all parents pray for.
♦ Reiki stimulates balance in the new born baby. It can easily be channelled to the baby whenever the mother or father (depending on who has been attuned to the energy) touches their child.
♦ Reiki can be used to help treat cradle cap, colic and wind. **Important Note**: *Always consult your doctor no matter how trivial it may seem if you are concerned about your baby.*

Children

- Reiki can be used to treat your children throughout their lives. From the early days and months through puberty, adolescence and into adulthood.
- Reiki is wonderful for all their aches and pains. Instinctively we touch or kiss better our children when they fall or injure themselves. With Reiki we speed up the healing process and boost their own natural healing abilities.
- Reiki is a special gift you can share with your children. We recommend you teach your own children the five principles of Reiki and have them incorporate them into their lives.
- Children love Reiki. If possible you should introduce and attune your children to Reiki. It will help them focus and find their own path in life.
- Use Reiki at bedtime to help your children drift off to sleep.
- Reiki balances your child's mind body and spirit leading to a clearer more focussed approach to life at school and at home.
- When a child has an accident they often cry because of the shock. Treat your child by Placing one of your hands on their solar plexus and the other at the base of the spine.

CHAPTER 15

REIKI BRINGS COMFORT TO THE DYING

There is only one certainty in life and that is that death comes to us all. Facing our own mortality is often difficult. We have two main choices in coming to terms with our own death or the death of a family member or friend. We can choose to view death as final and become consumed in grief or we can envisage life after death and celebrate the transition to eternal life. Our beliefs and personal experiences shape how we deal with this extremely emotive issue.

Losing my sister Kim at the young age of thirty-three was a devastating blow to myself and my family. It was the first time I had experienced losing someone close. Looking back in hindsight and through my own research and subsequent experiences with people who came to me for help before dying, I found many common attitudes and mistakes associated with death. The western world in general treats the subject of dying as taboo. Something we shouldn't talk about.

As a stark contrast, Eastern philosophy and the teachings and beliefs of many ancient cultures view death as a natural part of life. They believe that our souls are eternal. The body is only a temporary vessel that allows the soul access to Earth. Karmicly we are here to learn and grow.

When a person becomes more spiritually aware they grow to understand and accept these ancient beliefs. When you look at the two choices it should be easy to believe in life after death, rather than believe that death is final and we all have nothing else to look forward to. All religions are built on the premise that to obtain eternal life you must be good in this one.

Thanatology (the study of death and the dying) has given humanity the insight into life after death. People who have had near death experiences bring hope and reports of a better place. Books such as *Saved By The Light by Dannion Brinkley* offer inspiration and comfort to us all. In 1975 Dannion was struck by lightning as he made a telephone call to a business partner during a thunderstorm. He was pronounced dead in the ambulance on the way to hospital. For a little over twenty minutes he experienced what many people fear the most — **what really happens to you when you die**.

Dannion Brinkley tells how his ethereal soul leaves his earthly body and floats high above looking down at the scene of his death. He felt no pain or sadness at leaving his body or his life behind. A tunnel of bright light appears in front of him and he is quickly engulfed by it. As he progresses into the light he feels an overwhelming sense of peace and love. He goes on to tell of meeting spiritual beings and being shown a beautiful spiritual realm.

This life changing experience is not unique to Dannion Brinkley, thousands of other people who have died on the operating table or after an accident only to come back from the brink have reported similar experiences. If Dannion had been the only person to profess to such a profound experience then we could dismiss it as fiction or fantasy. A man with a wild imagination who suffered hallucinations perhaps after a serious and almost fatal accident.

There are nine common traits that thanatologists like Dr Raymond Moody (*author of life after life*) have been able to define through countless studies with people who have had near death experiences. This research proves there is life after death. The nine common traits are as follows:

1 A person senses they are dead.
2 A feeling of peace without pain no matter how they died.
3 An out of body experience. Their soul or essence floats above the dead body below.
4 A tunnel appears and the person is drawn into another world.
5 Beings of light appear, often deceased relatives and friends.
6 A particular being of light appears to greet and guide them.
7 The being of light takes them through a life review which highlights all the pleasant and unpleasant aspects of their life.
8 The person is told they must return. They feel reluctant to do so but understand they have no choice.
9 On returning the person has a personality transformation. They no longer fear death and are often guided and inspired towards a new definite purpose in their life.

The knowledge that there is life after death should be incorporated into your own life as well as the life of your family, friends and people who you meet along your path to eternal life. We urge you to study and become more aware of how to use this knowledge to help people who fear death. Make their transition a happy and joyous experience. Treat also their families so they may celebrate in the knowledge that their love-ones are not suffering and lost forever. They have simply migrated to a beautiful spiritual world that is filled with pure unconditional love. One day they will once again meet and be with them.

Working With People Who Are Dying

Reiki connects us to the universal life force. The energy and unconditional love that people who have had near death experiences talk about. When you use Reiki in a situation such as with a person who is terminally ill you are connecting them to the unconditional love of God and preparing them for their transition. You will often find Reiki temporarily revitalises them so they have the energy to deal with any unfinished business they may have.

It is important to help them if possible tidy up their affairs. Teach them to heal and mend any family relationships that may have been strained in the past. Encourage them to forgive and let go of any unnecessary anger and pain. Death is not failure it is a natural part of life. Encourage family members and friends to say goodbye and let the person who is dying know it's okay to go, and although it hurts they can survive and carry on without them. This often brings relief and removes the feeling of guilt from the person who is dying.

Reiki can alleviate pain and anxiety and bring final peace and harmony to the mind body and spirit. Reiki gives the person control of how and when they die. Reiki builds a bridge to the other side and brings the life of the person to a joyful conclusion.

Treat the family and friends if possible with Reiki after their love-one has passed on. We have found while the soul has departed and gone on to a joyous beginning the people left behind often find it extremely difficult to come to terms with losing a close family member or friend. Heal their pain and fill their mind body spirit and lives with the unconditional and omnipotent love of Reiki.

"When you were born, you cried and the world rejoiced.
Live your life in such a manner that when you die
the world cries and you rejoice."

Traditional Indian Saying

CHAPTER 16

USE YOUR IMAGINATION

Reiki is present in all living things. Your imagination is the only thing that can set limitations on its uses. We have listed some of the of the most common in this chapter.

Reiki And Animals

All animals adore Reiki. Large or small, fierce or friendly. Animals are extremely sensitive to the healing energy of Reiki. Start practising with your own pets and as you become more confident you can move onto other peoples pets and animals. As with treating humans Reiki will go where it is needed most. The only difference with animals is that they often guide you to the exact place that requires treatment by moving around until your hand lands on the exact spot. Animals will also let you know when they have had enough by moving away.

There is a huge market for treating animals. Use you imagination to develop your own techniques for treatment and develop a marketing strategy. Talk to your local vet or animal welfare centre. Advertise, you'll be surprised at the number of people with pets who need and want your help.

Basic Techniques For Animals:

♦ The very small animals such as birds or mice can be cupped in your hands.
♦ Larger animals such as cats, dogs, horses and cows normally prefer you to begin by placing your hands behind their ears and working around the body as with a normal full treatment for humans. However, if the animal has a specific injury place your hands directly over the injury.
♦ Fish can be treated by placing your hands on either side of the fish tank.
♦ Animals that are wild or dangerous can be treated safely through distance healing (second degree).
♦ Another safe way to treat animals is by treating their food and drink. However, this is a weaker form of treatment.

REMEMBER USE YOUR IMAGINATION

Plants And Vegetation

Reiki will enrich your plants, flowers, trees and gardens. Daily treatment will soon show positive results. The easiest way to prove how effective Reiki is with your plants and vegetation is to conduct a simple experiment.

Take several seeds, charge half of them with Reiki and place them in a pot. Then plant the other untreated seeds in a separate identical pot. Treat the seeds which were charged in the beginning with Reiki each day and observe how they flourish. Compare them to the pot of seeds that are simply left to grow naturally.

Basic Techniques For Plants And Vegetation

- ◆ Treat seeds or bulbs before sowing or planting by cupping them in your hands for several minutes.
- ◆ Indoor and outdoor potted plants can be treated daily by Placing your hands around the pot.
- ◆ Flowers, bushes and plants can be treated by placing your hands gently on their leaves, buds, branches or stems.

♦ Hold cut flowers by their stems for a couple of minutes. Continue daily treatment by placing your hands around the vase and you will extend the flowers life.
♦ Trees need longer treatments. The easiest way is to hug a tree.
♦ Lawns, plants, shrubs, flowers and trees can also be treated by treating their water supply.
♦ Larger gardens, woods and forests can be treated through distance healing (second degree).

Food And Drink

Treat your food and drink before you consume it. This will enrich it with the universal life force and improve the digestion process. The consumption of food takes more energy than any other bodily function. The quicker and more easily it is digested the more energy is available for other activities.

Basic Techniques For Food And Drink

♦ If you grow your own vegetables and herbs treat as shown previously for plants and vegetation.

- During food preparation you can place the food in your hands and conduct a short Reiki treatment.This is especially good if you are preparing a meal for the family.
- Just before you eat or drink place your hands just above the plate or glass. This is especially useful if you are eating out, and are unable to see the food being prepared.
- Alternatively you can place your hands on your stomach to assist digestion.

Further Uses For Reiki

There are a million and one other uses for Reiki including:

- Flat car batteries, especially on cold winter mornings.
- The medicine cabinet or first aid box.
- The Bath water.
- Your Home, your car.
- Protection while travelling on trains, planes, buses etc.
- Your work, letters, documents.

In fact you are only limited by your imagination!

Use Your Imagination Right Now By Listing As Many Ideas As You Can On Different Ways To Use Reiki In Your Life. Then Make Sure And Try Them Out. Each Idea Will Breed Another. Have Fun.... Good Luck.

CHAPTER 17

FINAL THOUGHTS

The first degree is the beginning of a wonderful journey filled with learning and growth on many different levels. Many people find that the first degree is all they need to study and learn to lead a more fulfilling life. The first degree connects the student to the universal life force and gives them the tools to heal themselves, their family and others.

Many people just like ourselves have been drawn to Reiki and find that it changes their lives. Reiki brings a sense of purpose, knowledge and direction into the lives of so many people. We have been able to incorporate the principles and teachings of Reiki into our lives and the other disciplines, practices and treatments we work with.

Reiki combines extremely well with all other therapies, including reflexology, aromatherapy, massage, the metamorphic technique, hypnosis, hypnotherapy, gestalt therapy, NLP, Dreamwork, regression therapy, focusing and crystal healing to name but a few. It also combines safely with orthodox medical care, particularly post-operatively health care, helping to accelerate the natural healing process.

Reiki is a special gift to be cherished and used. We urge you to incorporate Reiki into your lives and use this gift daily or as often as possible. Get busy and heal yourself, your family, your friends and others. Life is an adventure. Enjoy it.

Come to the cliff, he said.
They said, we are afraid.
Come to the cliff, he said.
They came.
He pushed them.
And they flew.

Unknown

REIKI
THE SECOND DEGREE

IMPORTANT NOTE TO THE READER

The second part of this book should only be studied by a student who is taking, or has completed the second degree workshop. Many people believe that the Reiki symbols should only be revealed to second degree students. ***Without the second degree attunement, the symbols are not effective.***

CHAPTER 18

THE SECOND DEGREE

Reflections

First degree Reiki is the beginning of an exciting and unfathomable journey filled with self discovery, personal change, love, growth, new experiences and a profound sense of bonding with a higher power. It takes most people from a position of scepticism and propels them into a new understanding of life. Reiki opens up doors to new dimensions, to things we never dreamt possible, and gives us access to the purest unconditional love available. Reiki is pure energy, it is omnipresent, omnipotent and omniscient. Reiki is available to all who wish to tap into it, accept it, and become one with its energy and wisdom.

Words cannot adequately describe Reiki, it needs to be experienced. Every person experiences Reiki in different ways, that is why it is impossible to define Reiki clearly in words. Whether you experience Reiki as a treatment from a Reiki practitioner or by attending a workshop, it will change your life for the better if you are open to the energy and allow it to envelop your mind, body and spirit.

THE SECOND DEGREE

The second degree is the next giant step towards understanding and becoming fully attuned to Reiki. Everyone attending the second degree workshop must have already completed the first degree. Students need to have been given the first degree attunements and the knowledge required to skilfully work with Reiki. Unlike the first degree, students should have obtained experience, skill and a level of intuitive understanding towards the unlimited power of Reiki.

Most second degree students no longer fear or harbour scepticism towards Reiki. They are normally enthusiastic and excited about the prospect of enhancing their skills and understanding. It is important to have taken time since the first degree workshop to assimilate and incorporate the teachings of Dr. Usui into your practice and daily life. Make sure you are attending the second degree workshop for the right reasons.

Like the first degree most people feel they are drawn at the appropriate time to the next level of Reiki. Often an event or strong feeling can direct you towards this new path. The main criteria for attending the workshop is that you personally feel ready to go forward with Reiki.

Trying To Understand How The Second Degree Works

It is almost impossible to explain how second degree Reiki actually works in a way that everyone can understand and accept it. To try to scientifically and logically grasp how the universal life force functions is beyond human intelligence. Like so many things in life, although we do not fully understand how they work we still use them to improve our lives.

Many people would find it extremely difficult to explain how electricity, televisions, faxes, computers, telephones and microwave ovens work for example. However, not being able to comprehend how they work doesn't stop people using them. Likewise, although no-one can completely explain how Reiki works it shouldn't stop you using and trusting in its ability to improve your life and the lives of the people you work with.

When you study, experience and work with the teachings and techniques of the second degree you will be able to make your own judgement on how you feel it works. Alternatively you could simply do what we recommend and just believe in its infinitive wisdom and let go of any doubts and fears.

However, for those who wish a brief insight into the second degree we will attempt to justly explain our own understanding of how the second degree works.

How We Believe Reiki Works

Reiki is omnipresent-present everywhere at the same time.
Reiki is omnipotent-absolute and infinite power.
Reiki is omniscient-infinite wisdom and knowledge.

The universal life force connects all living things together like a vast ocean. As droplets in this ocean we are communicating with and are connected to all other droplets in this ocean on an unconscious level. Similarly, every cell in the human body has its own individual position and responsibility. However, each cell is also unequivocally connected to and is unconsciously communicating with all the other fifty-trillion cells in the body. Deepak Chopra, in his book Quantum Healing also talks about how the entire universe is connected.

He explains how particles that are separated by immense distances of time and space know what one another are doing. When an electron for example jumps into a new orbit on the outside of an atom, the anti-electron (positron) paired with it must also react no matter where it lives in the universe. Each particle in our universe has an intelligence that communicates across time and space.

Scientists studying the behaviour of monkeys on the coast of Japan noticed one day a particular monkey had begun dipping his sweet potatoes into salt water before eating them. Shortly afterwards they found all the monkeys within the colony were also dipping their potatoes into salt water.

The scientist assumed the monkeys were just copying each other until they discovered monkeys in other parts of the world had begun dipping their potatoes into salt water also. The monkeys were communicating through an unknown intelligence across time and space. The scientists labelled this intelligent communication Morphic Resonance.

Interestingly another study found when giraffes began causing serious damage to trees by eating more of the tree than normal, the trees responded by increasing the amount of tannin in their leaves. This defensive action made the leaves too bitter for the giraffes to eat. Scientists discovered the trees were communicating with gases — an energy with intelligence. ***Likewise, Reiki is also an energy with intelligence.***

"If thou canst believe, all things are possible to him that believeth."

Mark 9:23

CHAPTER 19

NEW POSSIBILITIES

The second degree brings new possibilities. After the initiation ceremony the second degree practitioner is taught how to use the sacred Reiki symbols. These symbols are the keys that give the practitioner access to the full potential of the universal life force. There are three major new skills gained through the study of second degree Reiki. They are as follows:

♦ The Reiki practitioner can increase and focus the universal life force. This can be used for self healing or to heal others.

♦ The Reiki practitioner can complete a full Reiki treatment in about 20 minutes compared to the 90 minutes normally required by a first degree practitioner. The Reiki practitioner can now help more people in less time.

♦ The Reiki practitioner can send distant healing across time and space. Through the symbols the second degree practitioner can connect to another person or being anywhere in the universe — either in the past, present or in the future.

As you incorporate the Reiki symbols into your life you will find unlimited uses for them. The greater your understanding and imagination, the more varied applications you will discover and develop.

After the initiation ceremony the student will find that their personal vibratory level has heightened by as much as four times that of the first degree attunement. Their psychic abilities also increase by between 80-100%. As with all attunements the student will go through a 21 day detoxification process as their mind body and spirit finds equilibrium.

**The more I learn,
the more I live.**

Unknown

CHAPTER 20

THE SACRED REIKI SYMBOLS

The symbols are a very special and important part of Reiki. They are the keys that enhance and amplify the universal life force. Once the second degree student has studied and assimilated them, their healing abilities are immediately heightened. Without the second degree attunement however, they are worthless.

They were found in the Sanskrit sutras by Dr Usui. He realised during his time of fasting and meditation on Mount Kurayama that these esoteric symbols would enable himself and others to be finely tuned into Reiki, just like tuning a television or radio signal. The symbols were the tools he needed to focus the Reiki energy, enabling him and others to bridge the gap between the healer and the recipient, across which the universal life force could be drawn as necessary. These sacred symbols are also for self healing. They dissolve old destructive patterns, and increase the intuitive abilities of the student, while raising their conscious awareness and peace of mind to new heights.

Transcendental by nature, the Reiki symbols connect the practitioner and the recipient directly to the higher self or higher consciousness-the Rei. The symbols are similar to energy transformers they boost and expand the energy field. When a symbol is drawn or visualised in the outer realm it becomes a mirror image of another symbol on an inner realm. Simultaneously a connection occurs which has ramifications on all levels — inner and outer.

It is vitally important that at the moment of drawing the symbols the intention of the Reiki practitioner is absolutely clear and positive. Visualise or imagine the symbol as a live energy. Many see that energy as a white light. The symbols can be drawn mentally and transferred from the Reiki practitioners third eye on to the various chakra and hand positions on the recipients body. Some Reiki practitioners draw the symbols on the roof of their mouth with their tongue before transferring the symbols to a recipient. While other Reiki practitioners simply draw the symbols on their hands or the bodies of the recipient. If you are going to draw them, ensure no-one sees them.

CHAPTER 21

THE TRADITIONAL USUI SYMBOLS

The first symbol is the Cho-Ku-Rei pronounced cho-koo-ray. It is the power symbol and the activator. Often called "the light switch" as it turns on and activates all the other symbols.

- ♦ **CHO** - To cut. Remove illusions in order to see the whole.
- ♦ **KU** - Penetrating. Imagine a sword slicing through.
- ♦ **REI** - Universal. Omnipresent, present everywhere.

The Cho-Ku-Rei cuts through and removes resistance. In Japanese Cho-Ku means imperial command — immediate. The esoteric meaning of the symbol is dis-creation, illness and disease are creations being constantly recreated.

HOW TO DRAW THE CHO-KU-REI SYMBOL

Stroke 1
Draw a horizontal line from left to right.

Stroke 2
Draw a vertical line from top to bottom.

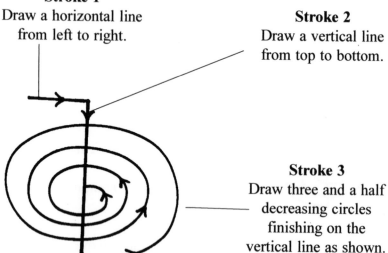

Stroke 3
Draw three and a half decreasing circles finishing on the vertical line as shown.

The Cho-Ku-Rei symbol dis-creates. This is the symbol that 'turns on' the second degree energy. Without this symbol the practitioner is still channelling only first degree energy. It can be used alone or as an activator for all the other symbols. Reiki's infinite wisdom will bring about whatever is needed.

How To Use The Cho-Ku-Rei Symbol

There are six main ways of transferring the Cho-Ku-Rei symbol from yourself onto your client. They are as follows:

◆ Visualise or imagine a brilliant white Cho-Ku-Rei Symbol projected from your third eye chakra onto the back of your hands as you rest them on the different hand positions of your client.

◆ Visualise or imagine a brilliant white Cho-Ku-Rei symbol on the palms of your hands before you place your hands onto your client.

◆ Draw the Cho-Ku-Rei symbol on the roof of your mouth with your tongue. Then project the symbol onto the back of your hands as they rest on your client.

♦ Draw the Cho-Ku-Rei symbol on the roof of your mouth with your tongue. Then project the symbol onto the palms of your hands before you place your hands onto your client.

♦ Draw the Cho-Ku-Rei symbol onto the palms of your hands using your index fingers. Then place your hands onto your client. (We always use Sai Baba's Vibhooti to draw the symbols onto the palms of our hands before each treatment.)

♦ Draw the Cho-Ku-Rei symbol in the air with your index finger in the direction you wish the Reiki to go.

Important Note: Never allow anyone to observe you drawing the symbols unless they are a second degree practitioner or a Reiki master.

To activate the symbols you have just drawn you must always silently intone the words Cho-Ku-Rei three times. The symbol will not work without the words silently intoned. If the situation calls for it write the problem down on a piece of paper and draw the Cho-Ku-Rei symbol over the top of the writing. Remember to silently intone the words Cho-Ku-Rei three times. Then place the paper in the palm of your hands for a few minutes.

Examples of Uses For The Cho-Ku-Rei (CKR) Symbol:

◆ The *CKR* turns on the second degree Reiki energy.
◆ The *CKR* activates all the other symbols.
◆ The *CKR* protects you on all levels.
◆ The *CKR* will bring about whatever is needed in a situation.
◆ The *CKR* cleanses energies in your home, office,crystals, car.
◆ The *CKR* brings balance into your life.
◆ The *CKR* can be sewn into your children's clothes.
◆ The *CKR* can be sent under a stamp on a letter.
◆ The *CKR* can be placed under a sticker on a gift.
◆ The *CKR* can be used on your food, drink, plants, animals etc.
◆ The *CKR* can be used to help your career. Draw in on your desk, under the cash register, documents, letters, the telephone, your diary, computer, contract pads, tax or VAT forms.
◆ The *CKR* can be used on airlines, trains, pilots, drivers etc.
◆ The *CKR* can be drawn invisibly under your doormat, under wallpaper, in cupboards, behind pictures, on your front door.

You are only limited by your imagination. As you incorporate the symbols into your life you will use Reiki on everything.

The second symbol is the Sei-Heiki pronounced say-high-key. This is the emotional and mental symbol used primarily for emotional and mental healing. Sei-Heiki balances the right and left brain.

♦ **SEI** - means birth, coming into being.
♦ **HEIKI** - means balance. Equilibrium.

How To Use The Sei-Heiki Symbol

The Sei-Heiki symbol can be transferred from yourself to your client in the same six ways already shown for the Cho-Ku-Rei (see page 129-130).

To activate the Sei-Heiki symbol you must first draw the Cho-Ku-Rei intoning the words Cho-Ku-Rei three times. You then draw the Sei-Heiki on top of the Cho-Ku-Rei and intone the Words Sei-Heiki three times. Finally you draw the Cho-Ku-Rei on top of the Sei-Heiki remembering to intone the words Cho-Ku-Rei Three more times. (see illustration on page 134).

HOW TO DRAW THE SEI-HEIKI SYMBOL

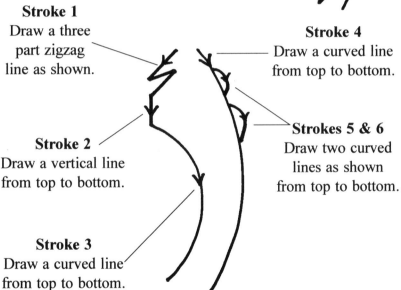

Stroke 1
Draw a three part zigzag line as shown.

Stroke 4
Draw a curved line from top to bottom.

Stroke 2
Draw a vertical line from top to bottom.

Strokes 5 & 6
Draw two curved lines as shown from top to bottom.

Stroke 3
Draw a curved line from top to bottom.

The Reiki Sandwich

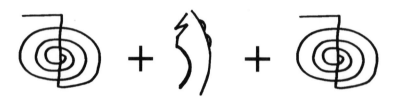

CKR + CKR + CKR + SH + SH + SH + CKR + CKR + CKR

In a situation where you feel your client is suffering from some sort of emotional or mental block the Reiki sandwich shown above can be used to release any blockages and allow the healing process to begin.

Visualise or imagine the Reiki sandwich coming out of your third eye chakra and entering the third eye chakra of your client. As you intone the words add the rider if it be for the highest good. Alternatively, draw the symbols on your hands and then place them over the clients third eye chakra. This is often needed when you are treating a person for addictions, weight loss or unwanted habits. Keep a box of tissues handy as this can often cause the client to become weepy and emotional.

The Reiki sandwich shown on the previous page can be used on all the normal hand positions. However, the third eye chakra position must be treated with the utmost care and responsibility. The Reiki sandwich will take the practitioner deep into the clients mind. It is vitally important to guard your thoughts as they can be picked up by the client. Ask the higher self of your client for consent before working on their third eye chakra. Your own intuition will give you the answer.

If you are treating a person who is suffering from a disease such as cancer, leukaemia or Aids visualise thousands of Sei-Heiki symbols penetrating every cell in your clients body.

When you find something you do not understand or you have a question that needs answering. Write it down on a piece of paper and draw the Reiki sandwich shown on the previous page over the top of it. Your answer will come to you intuitively.

Examples of Uses For The Sei-Heiki (SH) Symbol:

♦ The *SH* works on blockages and resistance in the body.
♦ The *SH* works on long-standing problems.
♦ The *SH* works on drink, drugs and smoking addictions.

♦ The **SH** works on anorexia nervosa and bulimia.
♦ The **SH** works on relationship problems.
♦ The **SH** works on nervousness, fear, phobias.
♦ The **SH** works on anger, sadness and other emotions.
♦ The **SH** works on grief from bereavement.
♦ The **SH** works on improving memory.
♦ The **SH** works on enhancing affirmations.
♦ The **SH** works on improving intuition and inspiration.
♦ The **SH** works on calming negative atmospheres.
♦ The **SH** balances energies in your home, work, crystals.
♦ The **SH** works on calming arguments.
♦ The **SH** works on improving poor communications.
♦ The **SH** protects you on every level.
♦ The **SH** Protects you from the losing personal belongings.
♦ The **SH** protects you while travelling.
♦ The **SH** helps you find lost articles.
♦ The **SH** improves creativity.
♦ The **SH** helps with coma patients, head injuries.
♦ The **SH** works on others as well as yourself.

Never use Reiki to manipulate others - misuse is one way of losing your gift.

The third Usui symbol is the Hon-Sha-Ze-Sho-Nen. This symbol is known as the distant or absent healing symbol, and is used to transcend time and space - past present and future. Like all the other Symbols the Hon-Sha-Ze-Sho-Nen (**HSZSN**) is activated by the Cho-Ku-Rei.

The HSZSN gives the Reiki practitioner the ability to channel Reiki across space, distance becomes no object. Reiki can be sent to a person across the room in a therapy situation or channelled to a person in another part of the world. The HSZSN also allows the practitioner to bridge time from the present to the past or future. Reiki can be sent back to heal a childhood problem or even further still to a past life.

Future situations such as operations, interviews or business meetings can be greatly improved by sending Reiki in advance. Time has no relevance when the HSZSN symbol is used.

HOW TO DRAW THE HON-SHA-ZE-SHO-NEN SYMBOL

When the Hon-Sha-Ze-Sho-Nen symbol is drawn all strokes are drawn from left to right and from top to bottom.

♦ The first horizontal stroke means number one. The beginning. Eternity begins in the moment.

♦ The second vertical stroke which crosses over the first one means number ten. The End. Completion. *The Japanese only count up to ten.*

♦ The third and fourth strokes combined with strokes one and two symbolise a tree in Japanese. Esoterically it means the tree of life and the tree of death and transformation, of knowledge, evil, desire and resistance. Also the tree of timelessness- it cannot die because it was never born.

♦ The fifth horizontal stroke means the root - the root of the tree. The cause, the essence, the origin. Strokes one to five combined form the first kanji - **HON**. (*Kanji* means Japanese writing using Chinese characters. *Kan* - Chinese *ji* character).

- The sixth horizontal stroke symbolises the land - the earth. Stroke seven a downward curving line means becomes - existence.

- Stroke eight is a vertical line drawn downwards from the curved line.

- Stroke nine is drawn from the left and curves sharply downwards as shown. (Strokes eight and nine combined look similar to a lowercase letter 'n').

- Stroke ten is a horizontal line drawn from the centre of stroke eight. The strokes eight, nine and ten form another Kanji which translated means the sun. ⊓

- Here we have the sun under the earth. Light coming into existence - the sun about to rise. Strokes six through to ten form the kanji - **SHA** which means a person that creates - i.e. a potter. A potter produces a vase from a lump of clay. He reveals the vase that was hidden in the clay. This symbol means what was hidden is brought into being. Bringing light onto the earth. The miracle of Reiki - when you place your hands on someone, you are revealing little by little what is already there.

♦ Stroke number eleven is drawn from left to right and seals the kanji as shown.

♦ Stroke number twelve is a vertical line drawn from the centre of stroke eleven downwards.

♦ Stroke number thirteen is a vertical line drawn as shown.

♦ Stroke number fourteen is a horizontal line drawn as shown. Strokes eleven to fourteen form the next kanji - **SHO** which means right, correct, justice.

♦ Stroke number fifteen curves downwards to the left as shown.

♦ Stroke number sixteen curves downwards to the right as shown. Stroke fifteen and sixteen combined form the kanji - **ZE** which means harmony. Acting appropriately, in the correct manner. Remember an energy with intelligence, it always goes where it is needed. Although the kanji **ZE** is drawn after the **SHO** it is spoken before it.

♦ Stroke number seventeen is a horizontal line drawn from left to right as shown.

♦ Stroke number eighteen is drawn horizontally from left to right parallel to stroke number seventeen. It then curves downwards and to the left as shown.

♦ Stroke number nineteen curves downwards similar to the letter 'c' as shown.

 ♦ Stroke number twenty also curves downwards similar to the letter 'c' as shown.

 ♦ Finally, stroke number twenty-one also curves downwards as shown. Strokes seventeen to twenty-one form the final kanji - **NEN** which means the heart, thought, also now -in the present moment in time.

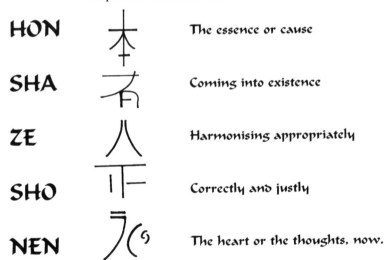

HON   The essence or cause

SHA   Coming into existence

ZE   Harmonising appropriately

SHO   Correctly and justly

NEN   The heart or the thoughts, now.

How To Use The Hon-Sha-Ze-Sho-Nen Symbol

The HSZSN symbol can be transferred from yourself to your client in the same six ways already shown for the Cho-Ku-Rei (see page 129-130). To activate the HSZSN symbol you must follow the same procedure used to activate the Sei-Heiki symbol - *The Reiki Sandwich.*

The Full Reiki Sandwich

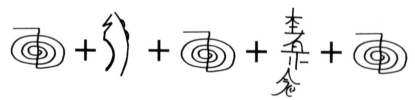

CKR+CKR+CKR+SH+SH+SH+CKR+CKR+CKR+HSZSN+HSZSN+HSZSN+CKR+CKR+CKR

ABSENT & DISTANCE HEALING

The three Usui Reiki symbols are the keys that unlock the doors to absent and distance healing. It is important to study and master these symbols. Practice drawing them until you can draw and visualise all three of them without referring to this book.

There are many ways to channel Reiki through the symbols. As you begin to practice and work with the symbols you will discover which method you prefer. It is not important to understand how it works. Belief and the right attitude make the real difference. Leave the logical sceptical part of your brain to one side and experience through practice how powerful and effective absent and distance healing can be. A wonderful way to prove to yourself that it works is to send distance healing to a friends sick pet. Animals are not influenced by hype. When you discover how you were able to treat an animal by sending Reiki through the symbols you will remove any doubts about its validity and concentrate on perfecting this profound form of healing.

The Surrogate Method

You can literally use anything as a surrogate to channel Reiki. The most important thing you must do is clearly specify that the surrogate is taking the place of whoever or whatever you are sending Reiki to during your invocation. Cushions, dolls, teddy bears, pens, photographs, crystals or the details of the person or thing written on a piece of paper are all good examples of a surrogate. Many Reiki practitioners have their favourite surrogate and use it for all their distance and absent healing. If you have a soft toy that you cherish try using that. A ball or small globe can be used as a surrogate to channel Reiki to mother earth. We always Reiki our car before each journey by using the cars steering wheel as a surrogate for the car. When we treat people using a surrogate we prefer to use a teddy bear as we are able to work more precisely on the various hand positions and chakras. For example if a person has a sore or injure left leg we spend more time treating the surrogate teddy bears left leg.

Let us assume for example you want to channel Reiki to your mother who is in hospital in another part of the country. Find a photograph of your mother. Write down her name, the hospital she has been admitted to and the ward on a piece of paper. Telephone your mother and ask for her permission to send healing to her. Choose a time between yourselves when you both will be able to relax and won't be disturbed. Place the photo and the piece of paper in your hands. If no-one is able to see or hear you make your normal invocation aloud adding also that the photo and piece of paper are to be used as a surrogate for your mother. Focus your attention on your mother and visualise or imagine her lying in her hospital bed or sitting in a chair depending on what you have arranged with her.

Holding the photo and piece of paper in your non dominant hand draw the Full Reiki Sandwich over the top with your dominant hand. Remember to intone the symbols and add the rider if it be for the highest good. Close your hands together and imagine sending healing light to your mother. Keep your hands closed for at least five minutes. As you become more experienced you will be able to intuitively work with the differing energy levels.

Once you have sent the Reiki take a moment to visualise or imagine your mother getting better. See her leave the hospital and make a full recovery. Trust in the power and wisdom of Reiki to make your vision into a reality. Complete the treatment by thanking the universal life force and any guides or helpers who assisted you in the treatment.

Remember the recipient is drawing the Reiki and doing the healing, you are just a channel. They need to be aware and ready to work with you in the healing process. Make sure they take the time each day to relax and are open to receiving Reiki. If the recipient is not able to spend too much time relaxing each day you can specify an agreed time for the Reiki treatment to last. All you need to do is write down the agreed length of time for the treatment on the piece of paper. This process like the normal full hands on treatment should be repeated at least four times over four consecutive days.

To save yourself time you can set up the four healing sessions in one go. Simply write on a piece of paper in addition to the recipients name and address the time and dates you wish the Reiki to be channelled to them You will only need to spend one five or ten minutes session channelling Reiki to your client so they receive it over four different days. Remember the symbols transcend time and space. As long as the recipient takes the time each day to tune into your Reiki signal they will receive and benefit from the universal life force.

Obviously the stronger your intent and the more time you spend sending Reiki the stronger and more profound it will be. Like all of the treatments the more practice and experience you gain the easier and stronger it will get.

The Thigh And Knee Method

Another method often used for absent or distance healing is the thigh and knee method. You will need to be seated to perform this treatment. Make your right knee and thigh the surrogate for the head and front of your client. Your right knee is your client head, your right mid thigh is your clients body and the rest of your right thigh is your clients legs and feet. The left knee and thigh represents the back of your clients head and body. Your left knee is the back of your clients head, your left mid thigh is your clients back and the rest of your left thigh represents the back of your clients legs and feet.

This treatment takes approximately fifteen minutes to complete. Using your left hand for the left knee and thigh and your right hand for the right knee and thigh work on the three positions for about five minutes each. Draw, visualise or imagine the three Usui symbols (*The Full Reiki Sandwich*) on each hand position. Remember to intone the words of each symbol three times. Complete the treatment as normal by thanking the universal life force and finally sweep your clients aura by rubbing your knees and thighs.

Visualisation Techniques

There are two basic ways of using visualisation to perform absent or distance healing. The first involves visualising or imagining the person you wish to treat with Reiki. For example let's assume you want to treat a close friend who is in hospital. Close your eyes and make your invocation. Repeat your friends name three times to focus your mind and establish a connection between yourself and your friend in hospital.

Transport your friend from the hospital and visualise or imagine them in a miniature form resting in the palms of your hands. Open your eyes and project the symbols from your third eye onto your friend resting in the palms of your hands. Alternatively, you can place your friend in one hand and draw the symbols over your friend with the other hand. Remember to intone the words three times and add the rider should it be for the highest good.

Gently cup your hands together. Keep your hands close for five to ten minutes or until you intuitively feel the treatment is complete. Open your hands and visualise or imagine your friend making a full recovery. Visualise or imagine a healing light enveloping your friend. Close your eyes and transport your friend back to the hospital. Say goodbye leaving the healing light with them to continue and complete the healing process. Complete the treatment by thanking the universal life force and make sure to wash your hands in cold running water.

Alternative Visualisation Technique

For this example lets assume you want to treat a friend's child who has chickenpox. If you also have children you probably don't want to risk infecting them by treating your friends child in person. Close your eyes and visualise or imagine being in your friends home. Have the child lie down on a bed or couch. Make your invocation and then project the three Usui symbols onto the child. Conduct a full hands on treatment. Visualise or imagine a healing light enveloping the child.

Say goodbye leaving the healing light with them to continue and complete the healing process. Complete the treatment by thanking the universal life force. Return to your home or office. Open your eyes. Remember to wash your hands under cold running water.

Examples of Uses For The HSZSN Symbol:

- The *HSZSN* works on deep seated diseases.
- The *HSZSN* works on long standing problems.
- The *HSZSN* channels Reiki to a person in another country.
- The *HSZSN* channels Reiki to someone in hospital.
- The *HSZSN* works on groups or large organisations.
- The *HSZSN* works on towns, cities and countries.
- The *HSZSN* channels Reiki to disaster or crisis situations.
- The *HSZSN* channels Reiki to world leaders.
- The *HSZSN* works on driving tests and examinations.
- The *HSZSN* works on interviews and meetings.
- The *HSZSN* works on karmic past life issues.
- The *HSZSN* works on children while they sleep or rest.
- The *HSZSN* helps treat patients with burns who cannot be touched or where there is a risk of infection through touch.
- The *HSZSN* heals the inner child.
- The *HSZSN* heals the past present and future.
- The *HSZSN* works on world peace.

You are only limited by your imagination. **Believe and succeed.**

CHAPTER 22

ADDITIONAL REIKI SYMBOLS

The three traditional Usui symbols cover every eventuality. They are omniscient and omnipotent. However, there are several additional Reiki symbols which have specific purposes and can be used in conjunction with The Full Reiki Sandwich. These additional symbols are not an absolute necessity. We believe the student should try using the additional symbols in their daily practice and decide for themselves whether they want to incorporate and use them in the future.

REVERSED CHO-KU-REI

This symbol is drawn in a clockwise direction unlike the traditional Usui CKR which is drawn anticlockwise. When used together the two CKR's are similar to the double helix found in DNA.

The double helix of the DNA is both clockwise and anti-clockwise. The chakras also radiate outwards from the centre of the body similar to the double helix with the narrowest section at the centre. The clockwise CKR connects with heaven while the anti-clockwise CKR connects with earth. You could experiment with both CKR's by using the traditional Usui CKR at the beginning of the Reiki Sandwich and the reversed CKR at the end of the Reiki Sandwich. You may find it brings balance and additional power to your work. If you do notice a difference you can incorporate it into your practice and daily use.

ZONAR

The Zonar symbol represents infinity, timeless, ageless, perpetual and eternal. It is drawn as the letter Z with the last stroke rising up into an infinity sign drawn three times across the centre of the Z. This symbol is used for past life issues and karmic and inter-dimensional problems that are difficult to define. Often there are problems and issues manifesting in our present life that are leftover remnants from a previous life or lives.

HARTH

This is the symbol for love, truth, beauty and harmony. It can be used to dissolve negative patterns we unconsciously use to insulate ourselves from the truth, thus 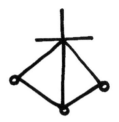 shattering delusion and denial. The Harth Symbol clears and opens the channels to higher consciousness. Often known as the master symbol as it is used in the initiation ceremony by the Reiki Master. *All strokes are from left to right, top to bottom.*

How To Draw The Harth Symbol

1)

2)

3)

4)

5)

6)

7)

8)

9)

FIRE DRAGON

This symbol represents the Ki energy travelling up the spine from the root chakra. It is used for spinal and back problems and is said to be good for the menopause.

To draw the fire dragon you begin at the base and draw an anti-clockwise spiral two and a half times. Continue the line upwards in a series of waves. Complete the symbol with a horizontal line across the top drawn from left to right.

JOHRE

The Johre symbolises white light. It is used to release blockages, for protection and to transfer healing white light. The symbol can be added to the Reiki Sandwich to send healing energy and protection across space and time. This symbol is difficult to draw so try to project the symbol from your third eye chakra. Draw from top to bottom as shown.

MOTOR-ZANON

Considered a Master symbol by Buddhist monks who use it for exorcism. Motor means to go in while Zanon means to come out. This symbol is used for viruses, infections and Aids. When the motor goes in, the little squiggle catches the virus or bacteria. The Zanon symbol is then drawn and it reverses polarity and leaves the body taking the virus or bacteria with it. Once you have drawn the Motor symbol draw both of the CKR's then follow with the Zanon symbol. **(CKR+CKR+MOTOR+CKR+CKR+ZANON+CKR+CKR).**

REN SO MAI

Pronounced LEN SO MY this symbol represents pure unconditional love and is used for emotional problems and situations. Normally placed over the heart chakra. Draw the figure eight (8) first followed by the dickie-bow shape.

DAI-KO-MYO

There are two versions of this symbol the traditional on the left and the non-traditional on the right. Use this symbol to heal the soul.

RAKU

This symbol is used for grounding and can be used at the end of each treatment

OM

Om is a Sanskrit symbol used for protection, healing and meditation.

REMINDER

- Always use the Cho-Ku-Rei symbol to activate all of the other symbols.
- Always intone the name of the symbol three times when you have drawn, visualised or projected it onto a subject.

CHAPTER 23

TIPS FOR WORKING WITH 2nd DEGREE REIKI

Empower Your Goals

Goals make the difference between success and failure in life. Reiki can empower your goals, dreams and desires. Write your goal on a piece of paper. Be specific. A goal should be set in the positive. Include all the facts, dates, names, etc.

Draw the full Reiki sandwich over the top of your goal. Reiki the paper for several minutes. Carry the piece of paper with you in your purse or wallet. Reiki the paper several times a day. Remember to add the rider should it be for the highest good. Believe and succeed.

The Magician *(Tarot cards)*

A simple way of sending Reiki is in the Magician position. Hold one of your hands in the direction you wish to send Reiki and the other pointing down towards the earth.

Preparation

Clear any negative energy and raise the vibration of the room by using the Cho-Ku-Rei symbol. Draw the CKR symbol on all the walls, ceiling, floor, healing couch, crystals and candles. When your client arrives project the CKR symbol onto their third eye chakra to relax and prepare them for a treatment.

Always draw the symbols on your hands before you begin the treatment (use Sai Baba's Vibhooti if possible). Visualise the symbols entering your clients body through each chakra and hand position.

Positive Affirmations

If you are working on a specific treatment try incorporating positive affirmations. For example if your client wants to stop smoking. Ask your client to silently intone at regular intervals throughout the treatment "I now release the need to smoke cigarettes." You should also intone the same affirmation on each new hand position. Pay particular attention to the third eye chakra. Remember the Sei-Heiki is used for addictions.

Alternatively, write the positive affirmation on a piece of paper and have your client hold onto it throughout the treatment. When the treatment is complete your client can take it home with them and keep it in their purse or wallet. Tell them to read it on a regular daily basis.

Scanning The Aura.

Before you begin a treatment scan your clients aura. Use your new heightened intuition to sense possible problems or blockages. Sense how the energy beneath your hands or in your palms feel. You may notice a variance in temperature. If you are guided or drawn to a particular position on your clients body go with it. Trust your intuition. Place your hands over that spot and work to heal and re-balance the distortion in your clients aura.

Zapping

When you use the HSZSN symbol you can zap people or situations from afar. Imagine your hand or finger is a laser gun and beam Reiki where it is needed.

Reiki And The Art of Focusing

Most people today are aware of the direct connection between the body and mind as it relates to health and well-being. We all store feelings and emotions over our entire lifetime in our bodies. When these feelings and emotions are left to fester they can invariably lead to unhappiness, sickness and disease. The bodymind has an early warning system designed to protect us from impending harm and danger. The signs normally express themselves as bodily aches and pains.

Instead of listening to the body's early warning system which is trying desperately to communicate most people take a pain killer to alleviate and suppress the ailment. Issues, emotions and feelings that need to be dealt with are lock away to cause physical and emotional damage. The body mind and spirit is thrown into state of imbalance. ***The cure for the pain is in the pain.*** Through the art of focusing we can communicate with the bodymind and release the blockages and destructive emotions.

Health, well-being and balance follows. Learning to communicate and understand your bodymind is vitally important in the search for longevity and happiness.

The Focusing Technique For Self Healing

Sit or lie down in a comfortable position. Close your eyes. Focus on your breathing. Begin a normal Reiki self healing treatment. Work from position 1 as illustrated on page 62 through to position 7 illustrated on page 65. When you have finish working on the heart chakra (position 7) rest both hands across your chest covering your heart.

Focus your conscious awareness inside. Place a microscopic version of yourself underneath your hands. Feel how safe and relaxed you feel. Allow the miniature version of yourself to travel all over your body from the tips of your toes to the top of your head. Notice any aches or pains that have appeared. If nothing appears straight away look again. Often you will find an ache or pain on the second or third run.

Place your full awareness into the pain. Focus and stay with it for a few moments. Say hello to the pain. Thank the part of the body that has come to talk to you today. Notice what colour it is? *(e. g, red)*. Notice what shape it has? *(e.g., square)*. If that part could communicate with you and could say only one word what would it be? *(e.g., sad)*.

Focus on the word sad (or any other word that comes up). Ask the word sad when it first entered your body. You will normally invoke a memory. ***Warning you may get tearful and emotional.*** You may want to cry, shout or scream — let it out. Continue the conversation with the part of the body until you have resolved the problem, emotion or issue. Use Reiki to heal. If you find it is too difficult to talk and continue the conversation send Reiki to the situation so it can heal it for you with its infinite wisdom. Complete session with the full self treatment.

On occasions you may find these issues are residues left over from past lives, childhood and times of personal loss and grieving. Use the full Reiki Sandwich to heal and remove the emotional and physical pain. This is an extremely powerful technique. Go carefully in the beginning until you have gain confidence and experience with it. If you find it too difficult to work directly with your various issues write them down on a piece of paper and send Reiki to them.

As you release the emotional blockages and residues you will feel a new sense of peace and well-being. ***Remember to heal yourself first***, then your family, then your friends and others. **This technique can be adapter and used to treat others also.**

Timeline Reiki

This technique is based on a mixture of Reiki and NLP (neuro linguistic programming). It allows you to travel into your future and create the life you want for yourself.

Sit or lie down in a comfortable position. Close your eyes. Focus on your breathing. Begin a normal Reiki self healing treatment. Work from position 1 as illustrated on page 62 through to position 7 illustrated on page 65. When you have finish working on the heart chakra (position 7) rest both hands across your chest covering your heart.

Focus your conscious awareness upwards towards the crown chakra. Visualise or imagine a small opening appear in the crown chakra. Float upwards through the opening and hover just above your body. (You may find you need to open your eyes to visualise or imagine.)

Look down and visualise or imagine your timeline. Typically you will see a line of images relating to past memories and future expectations. Normally the future projects forward while the past extends behind you. Whatever is right for you will appear.

Float gently above your timeline. Move forward until you reach the end of your timeline. If your timeline has ended before you can see that you have reached an old age or achieved your full potential project the Full Reiki Sandwich onto your timeline. Take hold of your timeline and stretch it out to add longevity, well-being and a rich fulfilling future.

Look back now along your timeline and review your life. See if you are satisfied with how you have lead your life. Did you reach your full potential? Did you make a worthwhile contribution to this world? Are you satisfied you lived your life to the full? Would you like to change anything about your life?

If you find a part (or parts) of your future timeline you want to change project the Full Reiki Sandwich onto that part (or parts). Visualise or imagine the infinite wisdom of Reiki dissolving the unwanted part of your future and replacing it with a new more positive, enriching and fulfilling part.

Look back along your timeline again and feel, sense, imagine, visualise a happier more fulfilling future. Envelop your timeline in the healing guiding light of Reiki.

Now look back at the wise old person you will become. Notice the *future you* has a gift for you. It may be words of wisdom or something that is very important to you on a personal level. Take your gift and give thanks to your *future self* for this wonderful present. Take a moment to assimilate and really appreciate this wonderful gift you have received.

Gently float back along your timeline to the ***present you*** reviewing your new future timeline along the way until you come to a stop above yourself in the present time. Look back into your past, see a younger you who once anticipated the ***present you***. Send Reiki back with its infinite wisdom. Then look into your future and see the *future you* who is expecting you. Send Reiki into the future.

Gently float back down through the opening in your crown chakra. Bring your awareness and your gift back down to your heart chakra beneath your hands. Place the gift you received from your *future wise self* into your heart chakra. Feel, sense, experience the new you. Use this gift wisely. Allow the process of *Tranceformation* and change to begin.

Complete the Reiki treatment by finishing all the self healing hand positions. At your own time and pace gently open you eyes. *Timeline Reiki can be adapted to be used with other people.*

"There is only one religion: the religion of love."
Sri Sathya Sai Baba

"There is only one Reiki."
Garry & Adele Malone

Tranceformational Seminars
Garry & Adele Malone

regular certificated workshops held
throughout London & the Home Counties.
(Other areas available by arrangement)

WORKSHOPS

First Degree Reiki
Second Degree Reiki
Master\Teacher Reiki
Hypnosis
Hypnotherapy
NLP
Dreamwork
Focusing

Past - Life Regression
Stress Management
Stop Smoking Start Living
Stop Drinking Start Living
The Food Combining Diet
Meditation
Visualisation
Success & Self Esteem

For further details on any of the workshops listed
above please contact Garry Malone
Tel/Fax - 01923 245181 Mobile 0958 443038
e-mail : garry.malone@virgin.net

Tranceformational Publications
Other Titles By

Garry Malone
MP.NLP C.M.H.C.Hyp REIKI MASTER/TEACHER

STOP SMOKING START LIVING   £ 9.99

STOP DRINKING START LIVING   £ 9.99

THE HYPNOTIC FOOD COMBINING DIET   £ 9.99

LIVING WITHOUT STRESS   £ 9.99

All the books above are in the same genre as The Essence of Reiki. They are concise, easy to read and understand. Using the latest proven techniques in the science of NLP and Clinical Hypnosis Garry will guide you to a new improved more controlled life. (Each book contains a FREE CD which contains powerful NLP and hypnotic techniques to ensure success)

For further details on any of the books listed above please contact Garry Malone
Tel/Fax - 01923 245181 Mobile 0958 443038 e-mail : garry.malone@virgin.net